KU-110-956

THE HOOPS
QUIZ BOOK

THE HOOPS
QUIZ BOOK

JOHN DT WHITE

APEX PUBLISHING LTD

First published in 2005 by
Apex Publishing Ltd
PO Box 7086, Clacton on Sea, Essex, CO15 5WN, England

www.apexpublishing.co.uk

Copyright © 2005 by John DT White
The author has asserted his moral rights

British Library Cataloguing-in-Publication Data
A catalogue record for this book
is available from the British Library

ISBN 1-904444-34-2

All rights reserved. This book is sold subject to the condition, that no part of this book is to be reproduced, in any shape or form. Or by way of trade, stored in a retrieval system or transmitted in any form or by any means, electronic, mechanical, photocopying, recording, be lent, re-sold, hired out or otherwise circulated in any form of binding or cover other than that in which it is published and without a similar condition, including this condition being imposed on the subsequent purchaser, without prior permission of the copyright holder.

Typeset in 10.5pt Times New Roman

Production Manager: Chris Cowlin

Cover Design: Andrew Macey

Printed and bound in Great Britain

*This Book is dedicated to the most loyal Celtic Fans I know -
Billy & Sandra Nolan.*

*Finally, a Special Tribute must also go to anyone who has ever pulled
on the hooped shirt of Glasgow Celtic Football Club, the late, Great,
Jock Stein, and to EVERY member of the famous Lisbon Lions.*

No Team will ever achieve what the Lions achieved.

FOREWORD

When John White first got in touch and explained about his quiz book, I must confess that alarm bells started ringing. All through my career, I have been asked to assess various books about Celtic, very few of which lived up to expectations. However, when John e-mailed me the details, I was very pleasantly surprised. This is an impressive piece of research.

John has put in an enormous amount of work to collect and collate all the different questions. Some of these cover all the famous moments in the club's long and illustrious history, which gives every Celtic fan the chance to learn more about the Hoops or merely refresh his or her memory.

In addition, there are various sections dealing with individual eras, players and managers, so no matter what age the reader is, there will be a subject he or she will feel comfortable with. The questions are well laid out and the answers easy to find.

All in all, the book is a welcome addition to the club's range of literature and will go down well with the huge Celtic support.

From a personal point of view, I did pretty well in answering many of the questions relating to Celtic's history and personnel from its inception in 1887 until around the year 1990. From then on, I did not star but, my goodness, reading the answers for that period has really improved my own knowledge of the last 15 years!

And don't forget, £1 from every copy sold goes to the Motor Neurone Disease Association, an organisation close to the heart of my old colleague, Celtic's Greatest-Ever Player, Jimmy Johnstone.

Jim Craig

INTRODUCTION

One thing and one thing only inspired me to write this book - Jock Stein and his 1967 Lisbon Lions. Even today it is incomprehensible to imagine ANY team winning Europe's top football prize for clubs, the European Cup (UEFA Champions League), with not only a team comprising of 11 players from the same country but a team whose players where all born within a short distance of the stadium they graced with commitment, honour, pride and professionalism for many years.

Incredible - certainly, Unbelievable - No. No because Celtic did it and let's face it the team they vanquished in the Final were far from nobodies. Inter Milan were revered across Europe having won 10 domestic Championships (no mean feat in Italian football), 2 European Cups, the Coppa Italia and 2 World Club Championships. And let's not forget that the only teams permitted to enter the European Cup in season 1966/67 were the Champions of their own country unlike today when up to 4 teams from the same country can be found diluting the competition.

Two others fact must not go unmentioned - this was Celtic's first foray into the European Cup and they also won every competition they entered in 1967!

In compiling my Book I must say thank you to the Webmaster at **www.sporting-heroes.net** for not only some excellent photographs but for assisting with some of the statistics about the players; the Webmaster at **www.soccerstats.com** for assistance in verifying trivia and the Webmaster at **www.keep-the-faith.net** for helping with data for a number of the questions I compiled. I would also like to express my thanks to David Ross, whose website www.scottishleague.net includes a regularly-updated question-and-answer section.

A special thank you must also go to Jeff Healey (Producer of "Lord of the Wing") and Jamie Doran (Director of "Lord of the Wing") who helped secure some wonderful quotes for my book.

And finally, I would like to thank Jim Craig and Paddy Crerand for the help, encouragement and support they gave me.

Yours in Sport, *John DT White*

THE BOSS - MARTIN O'NEILL - 1

1. At what Irish Football League Club did Martin begin his playing career?

2. What English Club did he join after leaving the Team in Q1?

3. What Club did Martin join in June 1981 and then left in February 1982?

4. Name the Team that Martin has played for in 2 separate spells with the Club.

5. Of what non-league "Town" was he appointed the Manager in August 1987?

6. Can you recall the Team Martin joined after he left the Club in Q4 for a second time?

7. At what "Wanderers" in the Conference did Martin's managerial apprenticeship effectively begin?

8. To what Division did Martin guide the Team in Q7 from the Conference in only 2 years?

9. Can you recall the Club that wanted him as their Manager in 1995 only for Martin to turn them down?

10. Of what Club did Martin become the Manager in 1995 after leaving the Club in Q7?

SEASON 2000-2001
TREBLE WINNERS

11.   By how many points did Celtic win the Scottish Premiership?

12.   What Team finished bottom of the league?

13.   To the nearest 10, how many points separated the Champions and the Team in Q12?

14.   What Team finished in 3rd place?

15.   Celtic recorded the highest league attendance of the season at Celtic Park. Who were the visitors?

16.   Celtic set the longest winning sequence during the season. How many games did this entail - 9, 10 or 11?

17.   The highest aggregate score for a league game was 8 goals and it happened 5 times. Name the Team that Celtic beat 6-2 in the league at Celtic Park.

18.   Celtic's best home win was 6-0 and they achieved this twice. Can you name either side Celtic beat?

19.   Celtic's leading goal scorer in all competitions was Henrik Larsson. Who, along with Chris Sutton, was Celtic's second-highest goal scorer in all competitions?

20.   What Team did Celtic beat in the Scottish League Cup Final?

HENRIK LARSSON - "THE MAGNIFICENT 7"

21.   In what year did Henrik sign for Celtic?

22.   What Celtic Manager signed him?

23.   From what Club did Celtic purchase Henrik?

24.   How many seasons did Henrik spend with the Club in Q23?

25.   What was the first trophy Henrik won with Celtic?

26.   In what year did he win the trophy in Q25?

27.   Can you name the Club Henrik played for before he moved to the Club in Q23?

28.   How many goals did Henrik score in his first season at Celtic Park - 16, 26 or 36?

29.   How many times was Henrik the Scottish Premier League's top goal scorer?

30.   How many Scottish FA Cups did Henrik win during his time at Celtic Park?

IF YOU KNOW YOUR
HISTORY - PLAYERS 1

31. Who captained Celtic when they beat Kilmarnock in the 2001 Scottish League Cup Final?

32. Name any 3 of the 6 Celtic players who are members of Scotland's Football Hall of Fame.

33. What Celtic player scored the winning goal of the game when Scotland played Brazil in the 1998 World Cup Finals?

34. A member of Celtic's 2003-2004 Championship Winning Team has a first name and surname both beginning and ending with the same letter, e.g. Sean Peters. Name him.

35. In what year did Brian McClair win the Scottish League Cup with Celtic?

36. Can you name the Polish player who played for Celtic in the late 1980s?

37. Who won the most caps for Scotland as a Celtic player, i.e. when he was a Celtic player and not at any other Club?

38. Name the Northern Ireland defender who missed a penalty for Celtic in the penalty shoot-out of the 1990 Scottish FA Cup Final against Aberdeen.

39. Can you recall the Celtic player who was voted the Scottish Footballer of the Year in 1973?

40. From what Portuguese Club did Celtic signed Jorge Cadete in 1996?

CHAMPIONS OF EUROPE

41.   In what year did Celtic win the European Cup?

42.   Can you recall the Italian side they beat in the Final?

43.   What was the score in the Final?

44.   Can you name any player that scored for Celtic in the Final?

45.   Who was the Celtic Manager that led them to European glory?

46.   What Czechoslovakian side did Celtic beat in the Semi-Final on their way to winning the European Cup?

47.   What was the name of the stadium where the Final was played?

48.   What affectionate nickname is Celtic's European Cup Winning Team better known as?

49.   Who played in goal for Celtic in the above Final?

50.   Was Inter Milan's goal in the above Final a direct free kick, an own goal, or a penalty?

PAOLO DI CANIO

51.   Can you recall the year in which Paolo joined Celtic?

52.   From what Club did Celtic sign Paolo?

53.   Apart from the Team in Q52, name 2 other Italian Teams that Paolo played for before he joined Celtic.

54.   To the nearest 5, how many games did he play for Celtic?

55.   What English Team did Paolo join when he left Celtic Park?

56.   Can you recall the name of the referee he pushed while playing for the Team in Q55 against Arsenal in November 1998?

57.   Apart from the Team in Q55, name 2 other English FA Premier League Teams that Paolo played for.

58.   What Football Award did Paolo win in 1997?

59.   Against who did he score the only goal of the game in January 2001 to knock them out of the English FA Cup?

60.   Of all the Teams he has played for, can you name the Team he scored the most goals for in a single season?

SQUAD NUMBERS - 1

ALL YOU HAVE TO DO HERE IS ASSOCIATE THE PLAYER WITH HIS CELTIC SQUAD NUMBER FOR THE 2004-2005 SEASON

61.	Didier Agathe	4
62.	Bobby Petta	18
63.	Henri Camara	5
64.	Neil Lennon	7
65.	Joos Valgaeren	11
66.	Stephen Pearson	16
67.	Stanislav Varga	17
68.	Ulrik Laursen	27
69.	Jackie McNamara	15
70.	Juninho Paulista	23

IF YOU KNOW YOUR
HISTORY - TRIVIA 1

71.   Apart from the Glasgow Cup, Scottish Championship, Scottish
        FA Cup, Scottish League Cup and the European Cup, what other
        trophy did Celtic win in 1967?

72.   What British Club, whose name begins and ends with the same
        letter, did Celtic meet in the 1965-1966 European Cup Winners'
        Cup?

73.   What "Inter" did Celtic meet in the 1st Qualifying Round of the
        1997-1998 UEFA Cup?

74.   Who, when he was appointed, became Celtic's 4th Manager in
        their history?

75.   After what famous American basketball player did Henrik
        Larsson name his son?

76.   In what season did Celtic prevent Rangers from making it 10
        Championships in a row?

77.   From what Club did Celtic sign Tony Mowbray?

78.   Can you name the English Premiership Manager (at the start of
        the 2004-2005 season) who was the joint-top goal scorer in
        Scotland with Celtic's Joe McBride in 1966?

79.   When Juninho signed for Celtic, there were only 2 vacant shirt
        numbers between 1 and 11. What were they?

80.   Who was the Celtic Captain that led the team to Championship
        success in the "10-in-a-row Busters" season of Q76?

LUBOMIR MORAVCIK

81. Can you recall the season in which Lubo joined Celtic?

82. In what country was Lubo born?

83. In what year did he represent his country at the World Cup Finals?

84. From what Club did Celtic sign Lubo?

85. In what country's league was Lubo playing when Celtic signed him?

86. What personal award did Lubo win in 2001?

87. Can you name either of the 2 French First Division sides he played for between 1996 and 1998?

88. How many goals did he score in Celtic's Treble Winning season 2000-2001?

89. Who were the opposition when Lubo played his last match for Celtic in May 2002?

90. When Lubo left Celtic, he went to play in the Japanese J-League for Ichihara. He teamed up in Japan with his mentor, who had Celtic connections. Name his mentor.

MOVING ON - 1

ALL YOU HAVE TO DO HERE IS ASSOCIATE THE PLAYER WITH THE TEAM HE JOINED AFTER LEAVING CELTIC (TRANSFER RELATES TO FIRST SPELL AT CELTIC)

91.	Henrik Larsson	Ipswich Town
92.	Regi Blinker	Leeds United
93.	Colin Healy	Ancona
94.	Tommy Johnson	Fulham
95.	Magnus Hedman	Everton
96.	Mark Viduka	Coventry City
97.	Mark Burchill	Barcelona
98.	Bobby Petta	Everton
99.	Alan Stubbs	Leicester City
100.	Steve Guppy	RBC Roosendahl

SEASON 1993-1994

101. In what position did Celtic finish in the league?

102. Apart from Rangers, name a Team that finished higher than Celtic?

103. How many points did Celtic finish behind Rangers - 8, 18 or 28?

104. What Team finished bottom of the league?

105. Celtic recorded the highest league attendance of the season at Celtic Park. Who were the visitors?

106. What was Celtic's heaviest home league defeat in an Old Firm game this season?

107. Can you recall the England striker who was the leading goal scorer in the league?

108. What "Pat" was Celtic's leading goal scorer in the league?

109. How many league goals did the player in Q108 score - 10, 12 or 14?

110. Name either of the 2 players who finished joint-second as Celtic's highest goal scorer in all competitions.

SUPER KENNY - 1

111. How many Championships did Kenny Dalglish win with Celtic?

112. Name any year in which Kenny received a Championship Winners' medal with Celtic.

113. How many times did Kenny win the Scottish Cup?

114. In what year did he win his only Scottish League Cup Winners' medal?

115. In what year did Kenny move to Liverpool?

116. How many First Division Championships did Kenny win during his time at Anfield?

117. Name any 2 seasons in which Kenny won a First Division Championship medal during his time as a player with Liverpool.

118. How many European Cups did Kenny win?

119. Can you recall any year in which Kenny lifted the European Cup?

120. With what Team did Kenny win the English Premier League?

LIAM BRADY

121. Who did Liam replace as the Celtic Manager?

122. In what year was he appointed the Manager of Celtic?

123. What was Liam's nickname during his playing career?

124. With what Team did he appear in 3 successive English FA Cup Finals from 1978 to 1980?

125. Can you recall the award he won in 1979?

126. What Italian Team did he join after leaving the Club in Q124?

127. Apart from the Team in Q126, name any other Italian Team Liam played for.

128. What was Celtic's highest final league placing under his management?

129. When he left Celtic Park, what English seaside resort-based Club did he become the Manager of?

130. Who replaced Liam at Celtic Park?

SCOTTISH CUP FINAL VICTORIES

ALL YOU HAVE TO DO HERE IS ASSOCIATE THE TEAM WITH THE YEAR CELTIC BEAT THEM IN THE SCOTTISH CUP FINAL

131.	Hibernian	1965
132.	Aberdeen	1972
133.	Rangers	2004
134.	Hibernian	1971
135.	Dundee United	1975
136.	Airdrieoneans	2001
137.	Dunfermline Athletic	1967
138.	Rangers	1988
139.	Airdrieoneans	1989
140.	Dunfermline Athletic	1995

ROY AITKEN

141.   In what season did Roy make his debut for Celtic?

142.   In what Division were Celtic when Roy made his debut for them?

143.   How old was Roy when he made his Celtic debut?

144.   Against what Club did Roy make his league debut for Celtic?

145.   What English Club did Roy join when he left Celtic Park?

146.   Can you recall the Scottish Team that Roy joined after a brief spell with the Team in Q145?

147.   Where in Scotland was Roy born - Arbroath, Irvine or Raith?

148.   In what season did he score his most goals for Celtic?

149.   How many seasons did he play at Celtic Park - 14, 15 or 16?

150.   At what Scottish Club did Roy end his playing career before later going on to manage this Club from 1994 to 1997?

THE "OLD FIRM"

151. In what year did Celtic last meet Rangers in the Scottish FA Cup Final?

152. What did the 5 Celtic players that played in a Celtic/Rangers Select Team against Caledonian FC on 11 March 1959 to mark the inauguration of Caledonian FC's new floodlighting system do before the game and then undo the following day?

153. Following on from Q152, name any 3 of the 5 Celtic (Rangers!) players that played in the game.

154. Following on from Q152, what Celtic player scored for the Celtic/Rangers Select Team in their 4-2 win?

155. Name the midfielder who was the only Scottish-born player in Celtic's starting line-up for the Old Firm match at Ibrox on 4 October 2003.

156. Prior to Mo Johnston, who was the last player to play for both Celtic and Rangers?

157. What "Andy" scored the only goal of the game when Celtic beat Rangers 1-0 at Hampden Park in the 1977 Scottish FA Cup Final?

158. How many times has Celtic met Rangers in the Scottish FA Cup Final?

159. What Celtic player, with the same name as a former Northern Ireland striker, is the only player to have scored a hat trick in 2 Old Firm Derbies?

160. Why did the SFA not award the Scottish FA Cup in 1909 when Celtic met Rangers in the Final?

LISBON LIONS - 1

161. Can you name the Lisbon Lion whose first name and surname both begin and end with the same letter, e.g. Sean Peters.

162. Who was Celtic's Captain when they lifted the European Cup in 1967?

163. Jimmy Johnstone was known as "Jinky" in Scotland, but by what nickname was he known in Eastern Europe as a result of his dazzling performances for Celtic across Europe?

164. What 4 trophies did Celtic win in the 1966-1967 season?

165. After their European Cup Final victory Jock Stein reportedly said that the only thing Celtic failed to win was the English derby. What player did he say would have won this famous horse race had he been allowed to enter it?

166. Name the Lisbon Lion that scored in 2 European Cup Finals.

167. When Stevie Chalmers scored for Celtic in the 1967 European Cup Final, how many goals had Celtic scored during the 1966-1967 season in all competitions?

168. Can you name the Lisbon Lion that won 2 English FA Cup Winners' medals with Newcastle United?

169. Who is the only man to have managed Celtic on 2 separate occasions?

170. To the nearest 10, how many Scottish League Cup appearances did Jimmy Johnstone make for Celtic?

PAT BONNER

171.   In what year did Pat sign for Celtic?

172.   Who signed Pat for Celtic?

173.   What was his nickname at the Club?

174.   What nationality is Pat?

175.   In season 1987-1988, how many domestic goals did Pat concede - 23, 24 or 25?

176.   Against what country did Pat perform heroics in the Second Round Penalty Shoot-Out of the 1990 World Cup Finals?

177.   To whom did Pat lose his first team place in season 1991-1992?

178.   To the nearest 10, how many caps did Pat win for his country?

179.   How many Scottish Championship Winners' medals did he win?

180.   How many Scottish FA Cup Winners' medals did he win?

THE SCOTTISH PROFESSIONAL FOOTBALLERS' ASSOCIATION PLAYER OF THE YEAR

*ALL YOU HAVE TO DO HERE IS ASSOCIATE THE PLAYER
WITH THE YEAR HE WON THE AWARD*

181.	Henrik Larsson	1991
182.	Paul McStay	2000
183.	Paolo di Canio	1980
184.	Chris Sutton	1987
185.	Davie Provan	2004
186.	Brian McClair	1998
187.	Charlie Nicholas	1999
188.	Paul Elliott	1997
189.	Mark Viduka	1988
190.	Jackie McNamara	1983

THE HISTORY OF CELTIC - 1

191. In what year was the Club formed?

192. What Team was the first Team that Celtic ever played, beating them in a friendly in Glasgow?

193. How many years after their formation did Celtic win their first major trophy, the Scottish FA Cup Final?

194. In what year did Celtic win the Scottish League Championship for the first time - 1893, 1895 or 1897?

195. What did Celtic win in 1907, the first time it had been achieved by any Scottish side?

196. What "Exhibition Trophy" did Celtic win in 1938 after beating Everton 1-0 after extra time at Ibrox in the Final?

197. What Scottish Team did Celtic beat 2-0 at Hampden Park in the 1953 Coronation Cup Final?

198. Why was the competition in Q197 held?

199. What "Cup" did Celtic win for the first time in 1956?

200. By what score did Celtic beat Rangers in the 1957 Scottish League Cup Final?

PIERRE VAN HOOIJDONK

201.   From what Dutch Club did Celtic sign Pierre?

202.   In what year did Pierre join Celtic?

203.   To the nearest £250,000, how much did Pierre cost Celtic?

204.   Against what Club did he make his Celtic league debut?

205.   How many goals did he score for Celtic in season 1995-1996 - 24, 25 or 26?

206.   What English Club did Pierre join after he left Paradise?

207.   Can you remember the Dutch Club that Pierre signed for after he left the Team in Q206?

208.   Name the Portuguese side he played for during the 2000-2001 season.

209.   Can you name the Dutch Club that Pierre won a UEFA Cup Winners' medal with in 2002, scoring twice in the Final?

210.   What Club was Pierre playing for when he scored the winning goal in a Champions League game on 15 September 2004?

I PLAYED FOR BOTH

ALL OF THESE PLAYERS PLAYED FOR BOTH CELTIC AND RANGERS. ALL YOU HAVE TO DO IS MATCH THEM UP WITH THE PERIODS THEY PLAYED FOR EACH

211.   Alfie Conn Jnr   Rangers 1904-06 & Celtic 1906-07

212.   David Taylor   Celtic 1907-09 & Rangers 1918-19

213.   Robert Campbell   Celtic 1917-18 & Rangers 1917-18

214.   Davie McLean   Celtic 1905-06 & Rangers 1906-14

215.   Hugh Shaw   Rangers 1913-18 & Celtic 1918-19 (Guest Player)

216.   Willie Kivlichan   Celtic 1984-87 & Rangers 1989-92

217.   Tom Sinclair   Rangers 1968-74 & Celtic 1977-79

218.   Scott Duncan   Rangers 1905-06 & Celtic 1906-07

219.   Maurice Johnston   Rangers 1905-07 & Celtic 1907-11

220.   James Young   Rangers 1906-11 & Celtic 1918-19 (Guest Player)

CELTIC v. EASTERN EUROPEAN TEAMS IN EUROPE

*ALL YOU HAVE TO DO HERE IS ASSOCIATE THE EASTERN EURO-
PEAN SIDE WITH THE YEAR AND THE EUROPEAN
COMPETITION IN WHICH CELTIC PLAYED THEM*

221.	1.FC Kosice (Slo)	UEFA Champions League 2003-2004
222.	Partizan Belgrade (Yug)	UEFA Cup 2002-2003
223.	Dinamo Batumi (Geo)	UEFA Cup 2003-2004
224.	FK Suduva (Lit)	European Cup Winners' Cup 1995-1996
225.	FK Teplice (Cze)	UEFA Cup 1996-1997
226.	Dukla Prague (Cze)	UEFA Champions League 1998-1999
227.	Partizani Tirana (Alb)	UEFA Champions League 2003-2004
228.	Croatia Zagreb (Cro)	European Cup 1979-1980
229.	FC Kaunas (Lit)	European Cup Winners' Cup 1989-1990
230.	MTK Hungaria (Hun)	European Cup 1966-1967

JUNINHO

231. From what Club did Celtic sign Juninho?

232. What Celtic legend's shirt number was he given upon signing?

233. Against what Club did he make his league debut for Celtic?

234. What is the only trophy that Juninho has won with Brazil?

235. Juninho made only one appearance for his country at the 2002 World Cup Finals. Can you recall the country he played against?

236. What Brazilian Club did he join in 1993?

237. Can you name the Brazilian Club he played for in 2000 when he won the Mercosur Cup and Brazilian League?

238. When Juninho first left the Club in Q236, what Spanish Club did he sign for?

239. While at the Club in Q238, Juninho spent loan periods at 3 different Clubs. Name any 2 of the 3.

240. In what year did he win his first International cap - 1993, 1994 or 1995?

THE BOSS - MARTIN O'NEILL - 2

241.　With what Club did Martin win a European Cup Winners' medal?

242.　In what year did Martin win his European Cup Winners' medal?

243.　To the nearest 5, how many International caps did he win for Northern Ireland?

244.　He was linked to becoming the Manager of what English Premier League Club during the summer of 2001?

245.　What Team has Martin both played for and managed?

246.　Who did Martin replace as the Celtic Manager?

247.　In what year did Martin become the Celtic Manager?

248.　What was the score of the game when Celtic first played Rangers under Martin's leadership?

249.　In what season did Martin lead Celtic to their first Championship success under his management?

250.　What Team were the second-last side Martin played football for?

SEASON 1996-1997

251. By how many points did Celtic lose the Scottish Premiership - 5, 10 or 15?

252. What Team finished bottom of the league?

253. Celtic recorded the highest league attendance of the season at Celtic Park. Who were the visitors?

254. With what Team did Rangers set the joint-longest winning sequence during the season of 7 games?

255. The highest aggregate score for a league game was 7 goals and it happened twice. Name any 2 of the Teams involved.

256. Celtic recorded the biggest home win in the league of the season. What Team were beaten 6-0 at Celtic Park?

257. Can you name the Celtic player who was the leading goal scorer in the league?

258. How many league goals did the player in Q257 score - 20, 25 or 30?

259. Who was Celtic's second-highest goal scorer in all competitions?

260. Can you recall what Team finished highest - Aberdeen, Dundee United or Hibernian?

TOMMY BOYD

261. At what Scottish Club did Tommy begin his Professional career?

262. What season was Tommy's first with the Team in Q261?

263. What English Club did Tommy sign for after leaving the Club in Q261?

264. Can you name the former Aberdeen Manager and the scorer of an English FA Cup winning goal that signed Tommy for the Team in Q263?

265. In what year did Tommy join Celtic?

266. What player left Celtic Park and moved to the Team that Tommy had just left as part of the deal that brought Tommy to Celtic?

267. What Celtic Manager brought Tommy to Paradise?

268. Against what Club did Tommy make his league debut for Celtic?

269. A possible move to what "Real" was Tommy linked with in the summer of 1996?

270. How many games did he play in his first full season at Celtic Park - 40, 41 or 42?

CELTIC PLAYERS IN THE BRITISH HOME INTERNATIONAL CHAMPIONSHIPS

271. Can you name the Celtic player who scored for Scotland against Northern Ireland at Hampden Park on 16 May 1973?

272. What Leeds United player replaced David Hay as the Scotland Captain when they met Northern Ireland at Hampden Park on 11 May 1974?

273. Apart from Kenny Dalglish, David Hay and Danny McGrain, name the other Celtic player who played for Scotland against Wales at Hampden Park on 14 May 1974.

274. Can you name the Wolverhampton Wanderers striker who came on as a substitute for Roy Aitken when Scotland lost 2-0 at Hampden to England on 24 May 1980?

275. Name the Celtic player who was a substitute for Scotland when they lost 1-0 to Northern Ireland at Windsor Park on 16 May 1980.

276. Name the Celtic player who was a substitute for Scotland when they beat Wales 1-0 at Hampden Park on 21 May 1980.

277. Name any 2 of the 3 Celtic players that played for Scotland in their 2-0 win over Wales at The Racecourse Ground, Wrexham on 12 May 1973.

278. Who made his Scotland debut in the above game?

279. Name the Celtic goalkeeper who played against England at Wembley on 19 May 1973.

280. Who was the only Celtic player to play in Scotland's 2-0 loss to England at Wembley on 1 June 1983?

FORMER CLUBS - 1

*ALL YOU HAVE TO DO HERE IS ASSOCIATE THE PLAYER
WITH THE TEAM HE LEFT TO JOIN CELTIC*

281.	Stephen Pearson	Feyenoord
282.	Jonathan Gould	Duisburg
283.	Ulrik Laursen	St Johnstone
284.	Henrik Larsson	Coventry City
285.	Mohammed Sylla	Paris Saint-Germain
286.	Lubomir Moravcik	Toulouse
287.	Dmitri Kharine	Atletico de Madrid
288.	Bobo Balde	Hibernian
289.	Stephane Mahe	Chelsea
290.	Daniel da Cruz Carvalho Dani	Motherwell

PAUL McSTAY

291. In what year did Paul sign for Celtic?

292. Can you name either of Paul's 2 uncles that played for Celtic?

293. In what year was Paul made Celtic Captain?

294. Who did he replace as Captain of Celtic?

295. How many Scottish Championships did he win?

296. Name any season in which Paul won a Scottish Championship Winners' medal.

297. What Football Club did he join after Celtic?

298. How many caps did he win for Scotland - 66, 76 or 86?

299. Can you recall any year in which he played for Scotland in the World Cup Finals?

300. In what year did Paul retire from Professional Football?

IF YOU KNOW YOUR HISTORY - PLAYERS 2

301. Name the Celtic player that was sent off against Rangers in the 1991 Scottish Cup Final.

302. What Club did Brian McClair join after leaving Celtic?

303. Can you name either of the 2 Celtic strikers who were the joint-top goal scorers in Scotland in 1989?

304. Name the 2 brothers that played for Celtic in the 1985 Scottish Cup Final.

305. Can you name the Celtic player who was voted the Scottish Footballer of the Year in 2004?

306. In what season did Henrik Larsson score 29 league goals for Celtic?

307. Can you name the Celtic player who was voted the Scottish Footballer of the Year in 2002?

308. Who in 1963 became the first Celtic player to score an away hat-trick in a European tie?

309. Against what country did Celtic's Charlie Tully score a corner for Northern Ireland?

310. What former Celtic player won a European Cup Winners' medal in 1978?

THE 1970s LEAGUE POSITIONS

*ALL YOU HAVE TO DO HERE IS ASSOCIATE THE SEASON WITH
CELTIC'S PLACING IN THE SCOTTISH 1st DIVISION/PREMIER
LEAGUE FOR THAT SEASON*

311.	Season 1969-1970	1st
312.	Season 1970-1971	1st
313.	Season 1971-1972	1st
314.	Season 1972-1973	5th
315.	Season 1973-1974	3rd
316.	Season 1974-1975	1st
317.	Season 1975-1976	1st
318.	Season 1976-1977	1st
319.	Season 1977-1978	1st
320.	Season 1978-1979	2nd

JACKIE McNAMARA

321. In what season did Jackie sign for Celtic?

322. Where in Scotland was Jackie born - Aberdeen, Dundee or Glasgow?

323. From what Club did Celtic sign Jackie?

324. To the nearest £100,000, how much did Celtic pay for Jackie?

325. In what season did he begin his Professional career with the Team in Q323?

326. What Celtic Manager brought him to Paradise?

327. Against what Team did Jackie make his Celtic league debut?

328. How many appearances did he make for Celtic in his first season at Celtic Park - 25, 26 or 27?

329. How many goals did he score in Celtic's Treble Winning season 2000-2001?

330. Up to and including the 2003-2004 season, under how many different Celtic Managers has Jackie played?

IF YOU KNOW YOUR HISTORY - TRIVIA 2

331.   What Irish Club, whose name begins and ends with the same letter, did Celtic meet in the 1986-1987 European Cup?

332.   Can you name the former Celtic Scottish International that has played for 3 Clubs that at some point in their history won the European Cup?

333.   Name any year in which Brian McClair won the FA Premiership with Manchester United.

334.   What Spanish Club did Celtic have to play behind closed doors in a European Cup Winners' Cup tie in September 1985?

335.   Following on from Q334, can you name the Austrian Team that Celtic played which, following disturbances at the game, resulted in UEFA making Celtic play their next European tie behind closed doors?

336.   What Team in the 1974-1975 season prevented Celtic from winning 10 Championships in succession?

337.   Who replaced Ronnie Simpson in goal for the return leg of Celtic's World Club Championship match against Racing Club in Buenos Aires, Argentina in November 1967?

338.   Who scored the only goal of the game in the first Old Firm match of season 2004-2005?

339.   Apart from Celtic, what other Team did Jock Stein take to the Semi-Final stages of the European Cup Winners' Cup?

340.   What Motherwell player scored against Celtic in his last ever game for Motherwell at Celtic Park and later joined Celtic?

CELTIC v. FRENCH AND ITALIAN TEAMS IN EUROPE

ALL YOU HAVE TO DO HERE IS ASSOCIATE THE FRENCH/ITALIAN SIDE WITH THE YEAR AND THE EUROPEAN COMPETITION IN WHICH CELTIC PLAYED THEM

341. Olympique Lyon   European Cup 1966-1967

342. Bordeaux   European Cup 1969-1970

343. Paris Saint-Germain   European Cup 1968-1969

344. FC Nantes   European Cup 1968-1969

345. Inter Milan   UEFA Cup 2000-2001

346. St-Etienne   UEFA Champions League 2003-2004

347. AC Milan   UEFA Cup 1999-2000

348. AC Fiorentina   European Cup 1981-1982

349. Juventus   European Cup Winners' Cup
                            1995-1996

350. FC Lyon   European Cup 1966-1967

JIMMY JOHNSTONE

351.   In what year did Jimmy sign for Celtic?

352.   What is Jimmy's middle name?

353.   By what affectionate nickname was Jimmy known?

354.   What did Jimmy have a distinct fear of?

355.   Against what Team did Jimmy score 2 goals to secure Celtic the 1967 Scottish Championship?

356.   How many Scotland caps did Jimmy win during his career - 23, 33 or 43?

357.   On how many occasions did Jimmy win a Scottish Championship Winners' medal with Celtic?

358.   How many Scottish Cup Winners' medals did Jimmy pick up during his career?

359.   In what year was he given a free transfer by Jock Stein?

360.   Under what Celtic Manager did Jimmy spend some time at Celtic Park as a Coach?

SCOTLAND'S LEADING
GOAL SCORER - 1

*ALL YOU HAVE TO DO HERE IS ASSOCIATE THE CELTIC
PLAYER WITH THE YEAR IN WHICH HE WAS THE LEADING
GOAL SCORER IN THE SCOTTISH PREMIERSHIP*

361.	Henrik Larsson	1967
362.	George McCluskey	1989 (Joint)
363.	Steve Chalmers	1982
364.	Tommy Coyne	2004
365.	Charlie Nicholas	1997
366.	Jorge Cadete	1991
367.	Mark McGhee	2001
368.	Pierre van Hooijdonk	1983
369.	Brian McClair	1996
370.	Henrik Larsson	1987

CELTIC PLAYERS IN WORLD CUP GAMES FOR SCOTLAND

371. Only 1 Celtic player played in all 3 of Scotland's games at the 1990 World Cup Finals in Italy. Name him.

372. Apart from Kenny Dalglish, David Hay and Danny McGrain, name any other Celtic player who played for Scotland against Czechoslovakia at Hampden Park on 26 September 1973.

373. What Celtic player, and future Celtic Manager, captained Scotland when they lost 1-0 to Czechoslovakia in Tehelne Pole, Bratislava on 17 October 1973?

374. Can you name either of the 2 Celtic players that played against Norway at Hampden Park on 15 November 1989?

375. What young Celtic player came on as a substitute for his teammate, Tosh McKinlay, when Scotland played Latvia in Riga on 5 October 1996?

376. Name any 2 of the 3 Celtic players that played against Zaire in Scotland's opening game of the 1974 World Cup Finals.

377. Which Celtic player captained Scotland in the 1990 World Cup Finals?

378. Apart from Tommy Boyd and Tosh McKinlay, can you name any other Celtic player who played for Scotland against Estonia at Rugby Park, Kilmarnock on 29 March 1997?

379. Can you name either of the 2 Celtic defenders that played against Belarus in Minsk on 8 June 1997?

380. Two future Celtic players also appeared for Scotland in the game in Q379. Name either of them.

CHARLIE NICHOLAS

381. In what season did Charlie make his debut for Celtic?

382. Against what Club did Charlie make his Celtic league debut?

383. What age was Charlie when he made his Celtic debut?

384. Where in Scotland was Charlie born - Clyde, Cowcaddens or Cowdenbeath?

385. How many goals did he score in his first season at Celtic Park - 14, 16 or 18?

386. In what year did he first leave Celtic?

387. When he left Celtic in Q386, how much, to the nearest £100,000, was the transfer fee that Celtic received for him?

388. What Scottish Premier League Club did Charlie join after he left Celtic for the second time?

389. For how many seasons did he play at Celtic Park?

390. In what season did he score 29 goals in 35 games for Celtic?

JOCK STEIN - THE LION KING

391. What was Jock's occupation before he became a footballer?

392. In what year did he join Celtic as a player - 1950, 1951 or 1952?

393. What Club did he manage after his playing career ended prematurely through injury?

394. Of what Club did he become the Manager after leaving the Club in Q393?

395. In what year did he become the Manager of Celtic?

396. How many times did Celtic win the Scottish League Championship under his management?

397. What English Team did Jock Stein briefly manage for a while after he left Celtic Park?

398. Of what Team was he appointed the Manager in 1978?

399. In what year did he tragically die?

400. What Team were the Team in Q398 playing when Jock suffered his heart attack and later died?

NATIONALITIES - 1

ALL YOU HAVE TO DO HERE IS ASSOCIATE THE PLAYER
WITH HIS NATIONALITY

401.	Henrik Larsson	Czechoslovakian
402.	Liam Miller	French
403.	Paolo di Canio	Belgian
404.	John Hartson	Swiss
405.	Bobo Balde	Swedish
406.	Ramon Vega	Danish
407.	Joos Valgaeren	Irish
408.	Colin Healy	Italian
409.	Lubomir Moravcik	Welsh
410.	Morten Wieghorst	Irish

JOHN COLLINS

411.   At what Scottish Club did John begin his Professional career?

412.   What season was John's first with the Team in Q411?

413.   In what year did John sign for Celtic?

414.   How many goals did John score in his first season at Celtic Park - 1, 3 or 11?

415.   In what season did John score his most goals for Celtic?

416.   What French First Division Club did John sign for after leaving Paradise?

417.   In what year did he sign for the Team in Q416?

418.   Can you recall the English FA Premier League Team he joined after leaving French football?

419.   How much, to the nearest £500,000, did the Team in Q418 pay for John?

420.   Apart from the team in Q418, what other English Premier League Team has John played for?

SEASON 1997-1998
10-IN-A-ROW BUSTERS

421. Name the Celtic Manager who won the Championship in this, his first season, at Celtic.

422. By how many points did Celtic win the Scottish Premiership?

423. What Team finished bottom of the league?

424. How many points separated the Champions and the Team in Q423 - 30, 32 or 34?

425. Celtic recorded the highest league attendance of the season at Celtic Park. Who were the visitors?

426. Celtic set the longest winning sequence in the league during the season. How many games did this entail?

427. The highest aggregate score for a league game was 8 goals and it happened twice. Name any 2 of the 4 Teams involved.

428. Who was the leading goal scorer in the league?

429. Who won the Scottish FA Cup?

430. Who won the Scottish League Cup?

44

LISBON LIONS - 2

431. Who was Celtic's Outside Right in the 1967 European Cup Final?

432. Who was the last Celtic player to score a league hat trick in an Old Firm game?

433. Who was Celtic's Inside Right in the 1967 European Cup Final?

434. Can you recall the Celtic player who was voted the Scottish Footballer of the Year in 1965?

435. Who was Celtic's Left Back in the 1967 European Cup Final?

436. How many goals did Jimmy Johnstone score in Europe during Celtic's 1966-1967 European Cup winning season?

437. Name the Celtic player who was placed 3rd for Europe's leading goalscorer in season 1967-1968 with 32 league goals.

438. Which of the famous Lisbon Lions sadly died on 27 April 2004?

439. To the nearest 10, how many Scottish FA Cup appearances did Jimmy Johnstone make for Celtic?

440. Can you name any 2 of the 4 Lisbon Lions that were the first Celtic players to be capped by Scotland after they won the European Cup in 1967?

SUPER KENNY - 2

441. Who did Kenny Dalglish replace as the Manager of Liverpool?

442. In what season did Kenny become the Player/Manager of Liverpool?

443. In what year did Kenny Dalglish resign as the Manager of Liverpool?

444. In what year was Kenny appointed Director of Football Operations at Celtic?

445. How much did Kenny Dalglish cost Liverpool - £440,000, £540,000 or £640,000?

446. Can you name the Liverpool Manager that signed Kenny Dalglish?

447. How many times did Kenny Dalglish win the Manager of the Year Award?

448. How many times was Kenny voted the English Footballer of the Year?

449. Can you recall any year he won the Trophy in Q448?

450. In what year was Kenny voted the English Players' Player of the Year?

FORMER CLUBS - 2

ALL YOU HAVE TO DO HERE IS ASSOCIATE THE PLAYER
WITH THE TEAM HE LEFT TO JOIN CELTIC

451.	Eyal Berkovic	Leicester City
452.	Craig Burley	Wimbledon
453.	Javier Sanchez Broto	Tottenham Hotspur
454.	Paolo di Canio	Livingston
455.	Neil Lennon	Aston Villa
456.	Stanislav Varga	Chelsea
457.	Ramon Vega	West Ham United
458.	Tommy Johnson	Bolton Wanderers
459.	Alan Stubbs	Sunderland
460.	John Hartson	AC Milan

RUNNERS-UP

ALL YOU HAVE TO DO HERE IS ASSOCIATE THE TEAM THAT PIPPED CELTIC TO THE CHAMPIONSHIP WITH THE SEASON CELTIC FINISHED RUNNERS-UP

461.	Season 1986-1987	Dundee United
462.	Season 1984-1985	Rangers
463.	Season 1983-1984	Rangers
464.	Season 1982-1983	Rangers
465.	Season 1979-1980	Rangers
466.	Season 1975-1976	Aberdeen
467.	Season 1954-1955	Rangers
468.	Season 1938-1939	Aberdeen
469.	Season 1934-1935	Aberdeen
470.	Season 1930-1931	Aberdeen

DANNY McGRAIN

471. In what year did Danny make his debut for Celtic?

472. Against what Team did Danny make his league debut for Celtic?

473. Can you name the Celtic Assistant Manager who first spotted Danny when he was playing for Scotland Schoolboys against England Schoolboys?

474. What part of his body did Danny fracture in an away game at Falkirk on 25 March 1972 that for a while threatened to end his career?

475. How many League Championship Winners' medals did Danny win with Celtic?

476. In what year was Danny appointed the Club Captain at Celtic Park - 1975, 1976 or 1977?

477. To the nearest 50, how many appearances did Danny make for Celtic?

478. How many goals did Danny score in almost 20 years at Celtic?

479. In what year did he appear in the World Cup Finals for Scotland?

480. What was he awarded in 1983?

CELTIC v. GERMAN AND BELGIAN TEAMS IN EUROPE

ALL YOU HAVE TO DO HERE IS ASSOCIATE THE GERMAN/BEL-GIAN SIDE WITH THE YEAR AND THE EUROPEAN COMPETITION IN WHICH CELTIC PLAYED THEM

481. Borussia Dortmund   European Cup Winners'
                           Cup 1984-1985

482. Anderlecht   UEFA Cup 1996-1997

483. FC Cologne   UEFA Champions League 2003-2004

484. Borussia Dortmund   UEFA Champions League 2003-2004

485. SV Hamburg   European Cup Winners'
                           Cup 1975-1976

486. KAA Gent   UEFA Cup 2002-2003

487. FSV Zwickau   UEFA Cup 1987-1988

488. Stuttgart   European Cup 1988-1989

489. Werder Bremen   UEFA Cup 1992-1993

490. Bayern Munich   UEFA Cup 1992-1993

TEAM NICKNAMES - 1

ALL YOU HAVE TO DO HERE IS MATCH CELTIC'S
OPPONENTS WITH THEIR CLUB NICKNAME

491.	Hibernian	The Sons
492.	Kilmarnock	The Livi Lions
493.	Hearts	Albion
494.	Dundee	The City
495.	Aberdeen	Rovers
496.	Livingston	The Hibees
497.	Raith Rovers	The Dons
498.	Brechin City	Killie
499.	Dumbarton	The Jambos
500.	Stirling Albion	The Dee

STILIAN PETROV

501.   In what Bulgarian city was Stilian born?

502.   In what season did Stilian sign for Celtic?

503.   From what Eastern European Club did Celtic sign Stilian?

504.   In what season did he begin his Professional career with the Team in Q503?

505.   How many goals did he score in Celtic's Treble Winning season 2000 - 2001?

506.   Against what "United" did Stilian make his Celtic league debut?

507.   How many appearances did he make for Celtic in his first season at Celtic Park - 25, 26 or 27?

508.   Up to and including the 2003-2004 season, under how many different Celtic Managers has Stilian played?

509.   In November 2002, Stilian was linked with a move to an Italian Serie A Club. Which one?

510.   In what season did he score his most goals for Celtic?

SEASON 1999-2000

511. By how many points did Celtic lose the league to Rangers - 17, 19 or 21?

512. What Team finished bottom of the league?

513. Celtic recorded the highest league attendance of the season at Celtic Park. Who were the visitors?

514. What was the highest number of goals scored in a league game?

515. Can you name either of the 2 Teams involved in Q514?

516. What Celtic player was the leading goalscorer in the league?

517. Who won the Scottish FA Cup?

518. Following on from Q516, what player was the second-highest goalscorer in the league for Celtic?

519. Celtic set the biggest league win in a game. Who did they beat 7-0 at Celtic Park?

520. Who won the Scottish League Cup?

CELTIC'S ALL-TIME LEADING GOAL SCORERS

ALL YOU HAVE TO DO HERE IS ASSOCIATE THE PLAYER WITH
THE NUMBER OF CAREER GOALS HE SCORED FOR CELTIC

521.	Bobby Lennox	192
522.	Sandy McMahon	235
523.	Jimmy Quinn	188
524.	Jimmy McGrory	167
525.	Kenny Dalglish	273
526.	Stevie Chalmers	470
527.	Patsy Gallacher	168
528.	Henrik Larsson	177
529.	John Hughes	217
530.	Jimmy McMenemy	232

DIANBOBO BALDE

531.   In what season did Dianbobo sign for Celtic?

532.   Can you name the Port City in the South of France where Bobo was born?

533.   For what country did Bobo play in the 2002 and 2004 African Cup of Nations?

534.   From what Club did Celtic sign Bobo?

535.   How much did Celtic pay the Club in Q534 for Bobo?

536.   Can you name the Club, where a Film Festival is held annually, that Bobo played for prior to joining the Team in Q534?

537.   Against what Club did Bobo score his first goal of the 2004-2005 Scottish League Campaign?

538.   How many games did Bobo play for Celtic in his first season at Celtic Park - 22, 32 or 42?

539.   At what French Club did Bobo begin his Professional career?

540.   Up to the end of season 2003-2004, how many goals had Bobo scored for Celtic?

MIXED BAG - 1

541.   What company was Celtic's shirt sponsor in season 1997-1998?

542.   What English Club has Celtic met in European Competition on 3 separate occasions?

543.   Who is the only Celtic player to have been capped more than 100 times by his country?

544.   Name the player signed in a "loan deal" on 31 January 2005.

545.   Can you name a former Celtic player with 3 letter "O's" in his surname?

546.   What was the first Trophy Celtic won under Martin O'Neill's leadership?

547.   Of what "Panel" was Lisbon Lion, Ronnie Simpson, a regular member after his Professional Career ended?

548.   In what position did Kenny Dalglish play for Milton Bank School?

549.   Name the Celtic player who was voted Scottish Football's Young Player of the Year in 1983.

550.   What company became Celtic's new shirt sponsor for season 2004-2005?

CELTIC v. PORTUGUESE AND DUTCH TEAMS IN EUROPE

ALL YOU HAVE TO DO HERE IS ASSOCIATE THE PORTUGUESE/DUTCH SIDE WITH THE YEAR AND THE EURO-PEAN COMPETITION IN WHICH CELTIC PLAYED THEM

551.	Sporting Lisbon	European Cup 1970-1971
552.	Sporting Lisbon	UEFA Champions League 2001-2002
553.	Go Ahead Eagles Deventer	UEFA Champions League 2001-2002
554.	Boavista	European Cup 1982-1983
555.	Porto	UEFA Cup 1993-1994
556.	Benfica	UEFA Cup 2002-2003
557.	Ajax Amsterdam	European Cup Winners' Cup 1965-1966
558.	Ajax Amsterdam	UEFA Cup 1983-1984
559.	Ajax Amsterdam	European Cup 1969-1970
560.	Porto	UEFA Cup 2002-2003

JOHN HARTSON

561.   In what season did John sign for Celtic?

562.   In what Welsh City was John born?

563.   From what Club did Celtic sign John?

564.   Can you name the London Club where John started his Professional career?

565.   What Club did he sign for during the 1994-1995 season?

566.   Against what Club did John make his league debut for Celtic?

567.   How many games did John play for Celtic in his first season at Celtic Park - 29, 30 or 31?

568.   How many goals did he score in the games in Q567?

569.   Against what country did John score for Wales in a European Championships Qualifier at the Millennium Stadium on 8 September 2004?

570.   Apart from the Team in Q565, what other London Clubs has John played for in the English FA Premier League?

THE SCOTTISH FOOTBALL WRITERS' PLAYER OF THE YEAR

ALL YOU HAVE TO DO HERE IS ASSOCIATE THE PLAYER WITH THE YEAR HE WON THE AWARD

571.	Danny McGrain	1969
572.	Billy McNeill	1987
573.	Henrik Larsson	1988
574.	Brian McClair	1983
575.	Craig Burley	1967
576.	Paul Lambert	1977
577.	Bobby Murdoch	2002
578.	Charlie Nicholas	1965
579.	Ronnie Simpson	1998
580.	Paul McStay	2001

THE HISTORY OF CELTIC - 2

581.   Who put Celtic out of their 3rd European Cup Semi-Final appearance in 1972?

582.   In what year did Celtic win their 9th consecutive Scottish League Championship?

583.   What Dutch Team beat Celtic in the Semi-Final of the European Cup in 1974?

584.   In what year did Billy McNeill first manage Celtic to Scottish League Championship success?

585.   Who replaced Billy McNeill as the Celtic Manager in 1983?

586.   What Team did Celtic beat to win the 100th Scottish FA Cup Final?

587.   Celtic won the 1986 Scottish League Championship against Hearts on goal difference. By what score did Celtic beat St Mirren on the last day of the season at Love Street?

588.   What did Celtic win in their centenary season?

589.   Celtic won their 29th Scottish FA Cup in 1989. Who scored the only goal of the game against Rangers in the Final?

590.   Who was the first person to manage Celtic without having ever played for the Club?

JORGE CADETE

591. What nationality is Jorge?

592. At what Italian Club did he begin his Professional career?

593. In what year did Jorge join Celtic?

594. What Celtic Manager brought Jorge to Celtic?

595. What Spanish Club did Jorge join after he left Paradise?

596. Can you remember the English Club that Jorge played for from February to June 2000?

597. Apart from Sporting Lisbon, can you name another Portuguese Team that Jorge has played for?

598. What Scottish Club did Jorge play for briefly during 2004?

599. In what African country was Jorge born?

600. During his time at Celtic Park Jorge was a member of Celtic's famous "Three Amigos" strike force. Name the other 2.

SCOTTISH CUP FINAL LOSSES

ALL YOU HAVE TO DO HERE IS ASSOCIATE THE TEAM WITH THE
YEAR THEY BEAT CELTIC IN THE SCOTTISH CUP FINAL

601.	Rangers	1990
602.	Clyde	1984
603.	Dunfermline Athletic	1956
604.	Rangers	1955
605.	Aberdeen	2002
606.	Rangers	1970
607.	Aberdeen	1966
608.	Heart of Midlothian	1973
609.	Aberdeen	1999
610.	Rangers	1961

THE BOSS - MARTIN O'NEILL - 3

611. Can you name the London Club in which Martin ended his playing career?

612. What Team did he captain to a "Finals" in 1982?

613. What type of injury ended Martin's playing career?

614. Name the non-league Club managed by Martin between his time in charge at Grantham Town and Wycombe Wanderers.

615. Martin led Wycombe Wanderers to 2 FA Trophy Final victories. Name either year he achieved this.

616. Of what "City" was Martin appointed the Manager before he took charge of Leicester City?

617. Can you name the former Aberdeen striker that Martin replaced as the Manager of Leicester City?

618. In what year was he appointed the Manager of Leicester City?

619. What London Team did Leicester City beat in a Division One Play-Off under Martin's leadership that saw Leicester City promoted to the FA Premier League for the first time?

620. What was the first Major Trophy Martin won in his managerial career?

PAUL LAMBERT

621.   In what season did Paul sign for Celtic?

622.   Where in Scotland was Paul born - Edinburgh, Glasgow or Motherwell?

623.   From what Club did Celtic sign Paul?

624.   To the nearest £250,000, how much did Celtic pay for Paul?

625.   Can you name the Scottish Club that Paul played for prior to joining the Team in Q623?

626.   In what year did he join the Club in Q625?

627.   Against what Club did Paul make his Celtic league debut?

628.   How many league games did Paul play for Celtic in his first season at Celtic Park - 26, 27 or 28?

629.   How many goals did he score in the games in Q628?

630.   At what Scottish Club did Paul begin his Professional career?

SEASON 2001-2002

631. By how many points did Celtic win the Scottish Premiership - 16, 18 or 20?

632. What Team finished bottom of the league?

633. To the nearest 10 points, how many points separated the Champions and the Team in Q632?

634. Celtic recorded the highest league attendance of the season at Celtic Park. Who were the visitors?

635. Celtic set the longest winning sequence in the league during the season. How many games did this entail?

636. The highest aggregate score for a league game was 7 goals and it happened three times. Name any 2 of the 6 Teams involved.

637. Henrik Larsson was the leading goalscorer in the league. Can you name his team-mate who was in 2nd place with 19 league goals?

638. Which Team won the Scottish FA Cup?

639. What "United" lost in the Final of the Scottish League Cup?

640. What Team did Celtic beat 5-0 twice at Celtic Park in the league?

PLAYER NICKNAMES

CAN YOU MATCH THE CELTIC PLAYER WITH HIS NICKNAME?

641.	Jimmy Johnstone	Jackie
642.	Pat Bonner	Choccy
643.	Bobby Lennox	Caesar
644.	Henrik Larsson	Yogi
645.	Billy McNeill	Fizz Bomb
646.	Brian McClair	The Magnificent 7
647.	Alan McInally	Shuggie
648.	John Hughes	Jinky
649.	Johannes Edvaldsson	Packie
650.	Dariusz Dziekanokski	Rambo

JOHAN MJALLBY

651.   What nationality is Johan?

652.   In what year did Johan join Celtic?

653.   For what home Club did Johan play prior to joining Celtic?

654.   How many years did Johan spend at the Club in Q653?

655.   Against what Club did he make his league debut for Celtic?

656.   Can you name the English Team that was interested in signing Johan in December 2003?

657.   How many league goals did he score in Celtic's 2000-2001 Treble Winning season - 4, 5 or 6?

658.   Can you name the Spanish Second Division Champions that Johan signed for in July 2004?

659.   In what year did he represent his country at a Major Finals for the first time in his career?

660.   What English Premier League striker did Johan say Henrik Larsson was better than in March 2003?

MOVING ON - 2

*ALL YOU HAVE TO DO HERE IS ASSOCIATE THE PLAYER WITH
THE TEAM HE JOINED AFTER LEAVING CELTIC
(TRANSFER RELATES TO FIRST SPELL AT CELTIC)*

661. Liam Miller   Hearts

662. Stephane Mahe   Norwich City

663. Eyal Berkovic   Preston North End

664. Vidar Riseth   Manchester United

665. Stephane Bonnes   Birmingham City

666. Olivier Tebily   Newcastle United

667. Pat Crerand   Partick Thistle

668. Jonathan Gould   Munchen 1860

669. Malky Mackay   Manchester United

670. Mark McGhee   Blackburn Rovers

NATIONALITIES - 2

*ALL YOU HAVE TO DO HERE IS ASSOCIATE THE PLAYER
WITH HIS NATIONALITY*

671.	Regi Blinker	English
672.	Tommy Johnson	Dutch
673.	Vidar Riseth	Israeli
674.	Johan Mjallby	Dutch
675.	Mark Viduka	Swedish
676.	Bobby Petta	Scottish
677.	Magnus Hedman	English
678.	Steve Guppy	Swedish
679.	Jonathan Gould	Australian
680.	Eyal Berkovic	Norwegian

RONNIE SIMPSON

681. Can you recall with what Scottish Club Ronnie, a Lisbon Lion, started his football career in 1945?

682. What age was he when he joined the Club in Q681 - 14, 15 or 16?

683. Against what Scottish League Club did he make his debut for the Team in Q681 - Celtic, Dunfermline or Hibernian?

684. For what Club did Ronnie's father play, winning many honours with them during his career there?

685. What Club did Ronnie join after leaving the Club in Q681?

686. Can you name the English First Division Club that Ronnie joined in February 1951?

687. Name either of the 2 Teams against which Ronnie won an English FA Cup Winners' medal.

688. What Scottish Club did he join after leaving the Team in Q686 and before he joined Celtic?

689. Who was the Manager of the Club in Q688 when he sold Ronnie to Celtic?

690. What else was Ronnie celebrating when he played his last game for Celtic, a 2-0 away win to Airdrie on 11 October 1969?

IF YOU KNOW YOUR HISTORY - PLAYERS 3

691. What Celtic player holds the record for having scored the most goals in European competitions for a Scottish Club?

692. Following on from Q691, whose record did the player overtake?

693. In what season did Brian McClair win his only Scottish Championship medal with Celtic?

694. What Celtic player, with the same name as a Newcastle United Centre Forward from the early 1970s, scored a hat trick for Celtic against Rangers on 10 September 1938?

695. Can you name the Bundesliga striker, who later played for Celtic, and who was the last Scottish player to score a goal in the British Home International Championship?

696. Can you name the last Celtic player to play in a British Home International Championship game?

697. Who was the last player to play for both Celtic and Rangers?

698. What former Celtic player won a European Cup Winners' medal in 1968?

699. Can you name the Scottish-born Celtic player who made his debut for the Republic of Ireland against Switzerland in 1992?

700. Who was the last Celtic player to win a Scottish FA Cup Winners' Medal and an English FA Cup Winners' medal?

IF YOU KNOW YOUR
HISTORY - TRIVIA 3

701.   What have Celtic and Sandy Shaw both got in common?

702.   Can you name the former Celtic Republic of Ireland International who has played for 3 Clubs that at some point in their history won the European Cup?

703.   What Manager left Hibernian after leading them to a Summer Cup victory and a 2-0 win over Real Madrid to take charge at Celtic Park?

704.   What company was Celtic's shirt sponsor in season 1998-1999?

705.   Name the Lisbon Lion who on 15 April 1967 became the oldest Celtic player to make his International debut for Scotland.

706.   Name the British Team that beat Celtic in the 1965-1966 European Cup Winners' Cup Semi-Final.

707.   What Celtic striker was sent off in the 2001 Scottish League Cup Final against Kilmarnock?

708.   Can you name the former Celtic and Northern Ireland Legend that died at the age of 75 in July 2004?

709.   How many league appearances did Brian McClair make for Celtic - 145, 155 or 165?

710.   Up to and including the 2003-2004 season, when was the last season an Old Firm Scottish FA Cup tie was played at Celtic Park?

NEIL LENNON

711. In what year did Neil make his debut for Celtic?

712. Against what Club did Neil make his Celtic league debut?

713. From what Club did Celtic sign Neil?

714. To the nearest £500,000, how much did Neil cost Celtic?

715. At what English Club did Neil begin his Professional career?

716. What Club did Neil join after he left the Team in Q715?

717. Name the Manager that signed him for the Team in Q715.

718. Can you recall the year in which Neil made his International debut for Northern Ireland?

719. What major trophy did he win twice with Leicester City?

720. Can you recall the country that Northern Ireland was due to play before Neil Lennon pulled out of the fixture after it was revealed that he had received a death threat?

CELTIC v. SCANDINAVIAN
TEAMS IN EUROPE

ALL YOU HAVE TO DO HERE IS ASSOCIATE THE SCANDINAVIAN
SIDE WITH THE YEAR AND THE EUROPEAN COMPETITION IN
WHICH CELTIC PLAYED THEM

721.   AGF Aarhus (Den)   European Cup 1971-1972

722.   HJK Helsinki (Fin)   European Cup 1973-1974

723.   B1903 Copenhagen (Den)   European Cup Winners' Cup
                                      1975-1976

724.   AGF Aarhus (Den)   European Cup 1972-1973

725.   KPV Kokkola (Fin)   UEFA Champions League
                                      2001-2002

726.   Valur Reykjavik (Ice)   UEFA Cup 2000-2001

727.   Rosenborg Trondheim (Nor)   European Cup 1973-1974

728.   TPS Turku (Fin)   UEFA Cup 1983-1984

729.   Vejle BK (Den)   European Cup Winners' Cup
                                      1965-1966

730.   Rosenborg (Nor)   European Cup 1970-1971

SCOTTISH FA CUP FINALS - 1

731.   How many times has Celtic been involved in a Scottish FA Cup Final that has gone to extra time?

732.   Name any Team that Celtic have played in a Scottish FA Cup Final that went to extra time.

733.   How many Scottish FA Cup Finals has Celtic won after extra time was played?

734.   Who beat Celtic on penalties in the 1990 Final?

735.   What was the score in penalties to the Team in Q734? - 8-7, 9-8 or 10-9?

736.   What Team was the first Team that Celtic beat in a Scottish FA Cup Final - Aberdeen, Queen's Park or Rangers?

737.   What Team was the first Team to beat Celtic in a Scottish FA Cup Final - Hibernian, Rangers or Third Lanark?

738.   How many Scottish FA Cup Finals did Celtic win during the 1960s?

739.   What Team was the last Team to beat Celtic in the Scottish FA Cup Final?

740.   Up to the 2004 victory, how many times have Celtic won the Scottish FA Cup - 34, 35 or 36?

MIXED BAG - 2

741.   Can you name the Brazilian striker who was released by Borussia Dortmund in May 2004 and spent a few days on trial at Celtic Park?

742.   With what Tottenham Hotspur player were Celtic linked in May 2004?

743.   What prominent UEFA Official was one of the men who urged Henrik Larsson to end his International retirement?

744.   Name the ex-Celtic player and Manager who managed Livingston during the 2003-2004 season.

745.   With what Team did Celtic only manage to draw 2-2 at Celtic Park on 3 April 2004 by scoring 2 goals in the last 7 minutes to save their unbeaten league record at home?

746.   Name either of Celtic's 2 goal scorers in the game in Q745.

747.   For how many games was Celtic unbeaten at home after the game in Q745 - 56, 66 or 76?

748.   What Team beat Celtic 3-0 at Das Antas Stadium in 2001 in a UEFA Champions League game?

749.   What country's FA was it reported in April 2004 that Paul Lambert had approached about undertaking a coaching course with them?

750.   Who was the first player that Martin O'Neill paid a fee for to bring to Celtic Park?

IN THE HOT SEAT

ALL YOU HAVE TO DO HERE IS ASSOCIATE THE MANAGER WITH THE PERIOD HE WAS IN CHARGE AT CELTIC PARK

751.	Liam Brady	1999-2000
752.	Jozef Venglos	1993-1994
753.	Jock Stein	2000
754.	Billy McNeill	1998-1999
755.	Lou Macari	1997-1998
756.	Wim Jansen	1994-1997
757.	Kenny Dalglish	1991-1993
758.	Jimmy McGrory	1965-1978
759.	Tommy Burns	1945-1965
760.	John Barnes	1978-1983

THE 1980s LEAGUE POSITIONS

ALL YOU HAVE TO DO HERE IS ASSOCIATE THE SEASON WITH CELTIC'S PLACING IN THE SCOTTISH PREMIER LEAGUE FOR THAT SEASON

761.	Season 1979-1980	1st
762.	Season 1980-1981	2nd
763.	Season 1981-1982	2nd
764.	Season 1982-1983	1st
765.	Season 1983-1984	1st
766.	Season 1984-1985	3rd
767.	Season 1985-1986	2nd
768.	Season 1986-1987	1st
769.	Season 1987-1988	2nd
770.	Season 1988-1989	2nd

TOMMY BURNS

771.   In what year did Tommy make his debut for Celtic - 1974, 1975 or 1976?

772.   Against what Club did Tommy make his Celtic league debut?

773.   How many seasons did Tommy spend at Celtic Park as a player?

774.   What was the highest number of league goals that Tommy scored in a season for Celtic?

775.   Name any season in which Tommy scored the goals in Q774.

776.   Can you recall the Scottish Club he led to promotion to the Scottish Premier League in 1992-1993?

777.   Tommy also played for the Club in Q776. What was unusual about his debut on 20 December 1989 against East Fife away for this Team?

778.   In what year was he appointed the Manager of Celtic?

779.   After losing to what Team was Tommy sacked as the Manager of Celtic?

780.   Of what English Team did Tommy become the Manager following the incident in Q779?

SQUAD NUMBERS - 2

ALL YOU HAVE TO DO HERE IS ASSOCIATE THE PLAYER WITH
HIS CELTIC SQUAD NUMBER FOR THE 2004-2005 SEASON

781.	Alan Thompson	9
782.	Stilian Petrov	33
783.	Mohammed Sylla	20
784.	Chris Sutton	10
785.	Paul Lambert	6
786.	John Hartson	19
787.	Dianbobo Balde	8
788.	Robert Douglas	12
789.	David Fernandez	3
790.	Ross Wallace	14

THE WORLD CLUB CHAMPIONSHIP

791.   In what year did Celtic take part in this competition for the only time in the Club's history?

792.   What Team did Celtic beat to qualify for participation in the competition in Q791?

793.   Who was the Celtic Manager at the time?

794.   Who were Celtic's South American opponents in a two-leg Final?

795.   What country did the Team in Q794 come from?

796.   What was the score of the game at Hampden Park?

797.   What was the score when Celtic visited the Team in Q794?

798.   What was the score in the Play-Off match for the World Club Championship between Celtic and the Team in Q794?

799.   Why did Ronnie Simpson not play in goal for Celtic in the Play-Off Match?

800.   In what South American city was the match in Q799 played?

BILLY McNEILL

801.   In what year did Billy make his debut for Celtic?

802.   To the nearest 5, how many trophies did he win during his Celtic career?

803.   When Billy left Celtic, at what Scottish Club did he take the Manager's job?

804.   What Scottish Premier League side did he manage after he left the Club in Q802?

805.   Name either of the 2 English sides he managed during his career.

806.   What was Billy awarded in 1976?

807.   How many times was Billy capped for Scotland - 29, 39 or 49?

808.   Who did Billy succeed as the Manager of Celtic?

809.   Against what Team did Billy score the winning goal in Celtic's 1965 Scottish FA Cup Final win?

810.   To the nearest 50, how many appearances did Billy make for Celtic?

SEASON 2002-2003

811. By how many points did Celtic lose the Scottish Premiership?

812. What Team finished bottom of the league?

813. Celtic recorded the highest league attendance of the season at Celtic Park. Who were the visitors?

814. Celtic set the joint-longest winning league sequence during the season. How many games did this entail - 8, 12 or 16?

815. The highest aggregate score for a league game was 8 goals and it happened 4 times. Name the Team that Celtic beat 6-2 at Celtic Park in the league.

816. Celtic recorded the biggest home win in the league of the season. What Team was beaten 7-0 at Celtic Park?

817. Can you name the player who was Celtic's third-highest goalscorer in the league?

818. Who scored the most European goals during the season for Celtic - John Hartson, Stilian Petrov or Chris Sutton?

819. Can you recall what Team finished highest - Hibernian, Kilmarnock or Livingston?

820. What was the score when Celtic met Rangers in the Scottish League Cup Final?

SCOTTISH LEAGUE
CUP FINAL LOSSES

*ALL YOU HAVE TO DO HERE IS ASSOCIATE THE TEAM WITH
THE YEAR IN WHICH THEY BEAT CELTIC IN THE SCOTTISH
LEAGUE CUP FINAL*

821.	Raith Rovers	2003
822.	Rangers	1995
823.	Aberdeen	2003
824.	Rangers	1973
825.	Hibernian	1965
826.	Rangers	1977
827.	Dundee	1991
828.	Rangers	1974
829.	Partick Thistle	1987
830.	Rangers	1972

VIDAR RISETH

831. What nationality is Vidar?

832. In what year did Vidar join Celtic?

833. What Celtic Manager brought him to Paradise?

834. Against what Club did he make his league debut for Celtic?

835. Can you name the Team against which Vidar scored the opening goal of the game in Celtic's 2000 Scottish League Cup Final win?

836. What German Club did Vidar join when he left Celtic Park?

837. Can you name the Norwegian Team that Vidar joined after he left the above German Club?

838. What season was his most productive for Celtic in terms of goals scored?

839. From what Austrian side did Celtic buy Vidar?

840. Against what Team from Luxembourg did Vidar score for Celtic in the 2000-2001 UEFA Cup?

WIM JANSEN

841. Who did Wim replace as the Celtic Manager?

842. Shortly after his arrival at Celtic Park, Wim purchased a goal keeper from Bradford City. Can you name him?

843. In what season did Wim lead Celtic to Championship success, thereby preventing Rangers from winning 10 titles in a row?

844. What Team did Celtic beat 2-0 at Celtic Park to secure the Championship in Q843?

845. Name either of Celtic's 2 goal scorers in the game in Q844.

846. What was the first Trophy that Celtic won under Wim's management?

847. What influential player did Wim bring to Celtic Park in November 1997?

848. When Wim arrived at Celtic Park he dramatically changed the Team, retaining only 3 regular first-team starters from the previous season. Name any 1 of the 3.

849. What defender did Wim sign from West Ham United to tighten up the Celtic defence?

850. With what Team did Wim win a European Cup Winners' medal as a player?

MOVING ON - 3

ALL YOU HAVE TO DO HERE IS ASSOCIATE THE PLAYER WITH THE TEAM THAT HE JOINED AFTER LEAVING CELTIC (TRANSFER RELATES TO FIRST SPELL AT CELTIC)

851.	Stephen Crainey	Liverpool
852.	Charlie Nicholas	Manchester United
853.	Ramon Vega	Derby County
854.	Didier Agathe	Livingston
855.	David Fernandez	NAC Breda
856.	Paolo di Canio	Southampton
857.	Kenny Dalglish	Watford
858.	Craig Burley	Sheffield Wednesday
859.	Lou Macari	Hibernian
860.	Pierre van Hooijdonk	Arsenal

NATIONALITIES - 3

ALL YOU HAVE TO DO HERE IS ASSOCIATE THE PLAYER
WITH HIS NATIONALITY

861.	Stilian Petrov	Irish
862.	Stephane Mahe	Russian
863.	Dmitri Kharine	Irish
864.	Neil Lennon	Dutch
865.	Alan Thompson	Scottish
866.	Pat Bonner	Brazilian
867.	Billy McNeill	Ivory Coast
868.	Juninho Paulista	French
869.	Mohammed Sylla	English
870.	Pierre van Hooijdonk	Bulgarian

EYAL BERKOVIC

871. At what Israeli Club did Eyal begin his Professional career?

872. What English Premier League Club did Eyal sign for after leaving the Team in Q871?

873. In what year did he make his debut in the English Premier League?

874. In what season did Eyal make his debut for Celtic?

875. Against what Club did Eyal make his debut for Celtic?

876. For what English Team was Eyal playing when Celtic bought him?

877. When he was with the Team in Q876, he had a fall-out with a team-mate who later signed for Celtic. Can you name the team-mate?

878. What English Club did Eyal join on loan during the 2000-2001 season?

879. Name the English Team that Eyal joined after he left Celtic.

880. For what English Premier League Team did Eyal play in the 2003-2004 season?

CELTIC v. UK AND IRISH TEAMS IN EUROPE

ALL YOU HAVE TO DO HERE IS ASSOCIATE THE UK/IRISH SIDE WITH THE YEAR AND THE EUROPEAN COMPETITION IN WHICH CELTIC PLAYED THEM

881.	Nottingham Forest	European Cup 1969-1970
882.	Inter Cardiff	European Cup 1970-1971
883.	Cwmbran Town	European Cup 1986-1987
884.	Liverpool	UEFA Champions League 1998-1999
885.	Liverpool	European Cup 1979-1980
886.	Leeds United	UEFA Cup 1983-1984
887.	Waterford United	UEFA Cup 1999-2000
888.	Dundalk	UEFA Cup 1965-1966
889.	Shamrock Rovers	UEFA Cup 1997-1998
890.	St Patrick's Athletic	UEFA Cup 2002-2003

SCOTLAND'S LEADING
GOAL SCORER - 2

ALL YOU HAVE TO DO HERE IS ASSOCIATE THE CELTIC
PLAYER WITH THE YEAR HE WAS THE LEADING GOAL
SCORER IN THE SCOTTISH PREMIERSHIP

891.	Henrik Larsson	1989 (Joint)
892.	Brian McClair	1966
893.	Kenny Dalglish	2000
894.	Joe McBride	1971
895.	Mark Viduka	1968
896.	Frank McGarvey	1999
897.	Charlie Nicholas	1981
898.	Harry Hood	1984
899.	Bobby Lennox	2002
900.	Henrik Larsson	1976

BRIAN McCLAIR

901. Where in Scotland was Brian born - Airdrie, Dundee or Glasgow?

902. With what English Club did Brian begin his Professional career?

903. Can you name the Scottish Club that Brian joined after leaving the Team in Q902?

904. What was the first Trophy that Brian won with Celtic?

905. How many Scottish Championships did Brian win during his time at Celtic Park?

906. How many goals did Brian score for Celtic - 99, 100 or 101?

907. To the nearest £50,000, how much did Manchester United pay Celtic for him?

908. How many league goals did he score in his first season at Old Trafford?

909. How many English Premier League titles did he win at Old Trafford?

910. Against what Team did he score the only goal of the game for Manchester United in the 1992 League Cup Final?

TEAM NICKNAMES - 2

ALL YOU HAVE TO DO HERE IS MATCH CELTIC'S OPPONENTS WITH THEIR CLUB NICKNAME

911.	Motherwell	The Saints
912.	Dunfermline Athletic	Gers
913.	St Johnstone	The Well
914.	Dundee United	The Accies
915.	St Mirren	Caley Thistle
916.	Partick Thistle	The Terrors
917.	Rangers	The County
918.	Inverness Caledonian Thistle	The Buddies
919.	Hamilton Academical	The East Enders
920.	Ross County	The Jags

SCOTTISH LEAGUE CUP
FINAL VICTORIES

ALL YOU HAVE TO DO HERE IS ASSOCIATE THE TEAM WITH THE
YEAR CELTIC BEAT THEM IN THE SCOTTISH LEAGUE CUP FINAL

921.	Kilmarnock	1969
922.	Hibernian	2000
923.	Dundee United	1966
924.	Aberdeen	1968
925.	Rangers	2001
926.	Hibernian	1957
927.	Dundee	1975
928.	Rangers	1970
929.	St Johnstone	1998
930.	Partick Thistle	1983

TOMMY JOHNSON

931. At what lower English League Division Club did Tommy begin his Professional career?

932. In what year did Tommy join Celtic?

933. From what English Premier League Club did Celtic sign Tommy?

934. Can you remember the English Midlands' Club that Tommy played for in between the Teams in Q931 and Q933?

935. To the nearest £500,000, how much did Celtic pay for Tommy?

936. Name the Celtic Manager who brought Tommy to Celtic Park, his last signing as the Celtic Manager.

937. In what Cup Final during 2000 did he score the last goal of the game?

938. Against what 'Rovers' did he make his debut for Celtic?

939. What English Premier League side did he join on loan during the 1999-2000 season?

940. When Tommy left Celtic Park on 6 September 2001, he was given a free transfer. Name the Yorkshire Club he joined.

IF YOU KNOW YOUR HISTORY - PLAYERS 4

941.   What Manager of an English FA Premier League Team at the start of the 2004-2005 season won a Championship medal with Celtic in 1981-1982?

942.   Who was the last teenager to score for Celtic in the Scottish FA Cup Final?

943.   Can you recall the Celtic striker who was voted the Scottish Footballer of the Year in 1987?

944.   Name any 2 of the 4 Celtic players that played in the last ever Scottish League v. League of Ireland game at Celtic Park in September 1970.

945.   How many Scottish Championship Winners' medals did Henrik Larsson win?

946.   What legendary Celtic player spent periods on loan at Glasgow Rangers and Stirling Albion during the 1950s?

947.   What future Celtic Manager was the unused Celtic substitute when Celtic beat Rangers 1-0 at Hampden Park in the 1977 Scottish FA Cup Final?

948.   Who was the last player to score a hat trick in an Old Firm game?

949.   Who was the last Celtic player to score in successive Scottish FA Cup Finals when he scored against Rangers in 1971 (Replay) and Hibernian in 1972?

950.   What Celtic striker was the first non-Scottish-born player to score a hat trick in a Scottish Cup Final?

IF YOU KNOW YOUR HISTORY - TRIVIA 4

951.   Who was the first non-Catholic Manager of Celtic?

952.   In what season did Henrik Larsson win his first Scottish Championship Winners' medal?

953.   Can you recall the Celtic player who was voted the Scottish Footballer of the Year in 1988?

954.   Name the Croatian Club from which Celtic signed Mark Viduka in 1998?

955.   In what year did Brian McClair leave Celtic Park?

956.   Who was the first Bulgarian footballer to play for Celtic?

957.   Who was Celtic's Manager when they won the Scottish League Cup Final in 2000?

958.   What company was Celtic's shirt sponsor in season 1983-1984?

959.   Can you name the Celtic defender who during his first season at Celtic Park went to the African Nations Cup with the Ivory Coast and ended up being held at gunpoint by the country's military following a series of poor results?

960.   Over the space of 3 days during 1993, Celtic had 3 different Managers. Name any 2 of the 3.

ALAN THOMPSON

961. In what season did Alan sign for Celtic?

962. Where in England was Alan born - Newcastle, Stoke or Wolverhampton?

963. From what Club did Celtic sign Alan?

964. To the nearest £250,000, how much did Celtic pay for Alan?

965. Can you name the English Club that Alan played for prior to joining the Team in Q963?

966. To the nearest £750,000, how much did the Team in Q963 pay for Alan?

967. At what then English Second Division Team did Alan begin his Professional career?

968. In what season did he begin his Professional career?

969. Against what Team did Alan make his league debut for Celtic?

970. Against what Team did Alan score his first league goal of the 2004-2005 season?

HENRI CAMARA

971.   From what Club did Henri join Celtic in a loan deal?

972.   What nationality is Henri?

973.   In what city, beginning with the letter "D", was he born?

974.   Can you name the French Club that Henri played for prior to joining the Team in Q971?

975.   Name any Swiss Club that Henri has played for.

976.   Apart from the Team in Q974, what other French Club has Henri played for?

977.   In what Cup Competition did he play for his country during 2004?

978.   Against what Club did Henri score his first league goal for Celtic?

979.   How many league games did Henri play for the Team in Q971 during season 2003-2004 - 28, 30 or 32?

980.   How many goals did he score in the games in Q979?

LISBON LIONS - 3

981.   Apart from Jimmy Johnstone, which other member of the Lisbon Lions has a first name and surname that both begin with the same letter?

982.   Can you name the famous England goalkeeper that paid a moving tribute to Celtic's Lisbon Lion, Ronnie Simpson, during the Celtic legend's funeral in April 2004?

983.   Who was Celtic's Right Half in the 1967 European Cup Final?

984.   Who was the last Celtic player to score a hat trick in an Old Firm game?

985.   Can you recall the Celtic player who was voted the Scottish Footballer of the Year in 1967?

986.   Who was Celtic's Right Back in the 1967 European Cup Final?

987.   Who was Celtic's Outside Left in the 1967 European Cup Final?

988.   Who did Jock Stein once describe as the player who had given him more headaches with his off-the-field antics than any other player?

989.   Who was Celtic's Centre Forward in the 1967 European Cup Final?

990.   Can you name the Lisbon Lion who is the third-highest scorer of goals in European competitions for a Scottish Club?

THE BOSS - MARTIN O'NEILL - 4

991. Where in Northern Ireland was Martin born?

992. In what year did he make his debut for Northern Ireland - 1971, 1972 or 1973?

993. Against what European Team did he make his International debut?

994. What was the first major trophy that Martin won with Nottingham Forest?

995. In what year did he win a League Championship Winners' medal with Nottingham Forest?

996. Name the Team that Nottingham Forest beat in the European Cup Final when Martin won his European Cup Winners' medal.

997. To the nearest 50, how many appearances did he make for Nottingham Forest?

998. In what year did Martin win his last International Cap for Northern Ireland?

999. Who were Northern Ireland's Scandinavian opponents in the game in Q998?

1000. In what year did Martin lead Wycombe Wanderers to a "Double" success in the GM Vauxhall Conference Championship and the FA Trophy Vase?

ALAN STUBBS

1001. At what English Club did Alan begin his Professional career?

1002. What season was Alan's first with the Team in Q1001?

1003. In what year did Alan sign for Celtic?

1004. Can you name the Celtic Manager who signed Alan?

1005. To the nearest £500,000, how much did Celtic pay for Alan?

1006. How many Scottish League Championship Winners' medals did Alan win?

1007. How many league goals did he score during Celtic's 2000-2001 Treble Winning season?

1008. In what year did he leave Celtic Park?

1009. Can you name the English Premier League Team that he joined after leaving Celtic?

1010. What former Rangers defender did he replace at the Team in Q1009?

FORMER CLUBS - 3

ALL YOU HAVE TO DO HERE IS ASSOCIATE THE PLAYER
WITH THE TEAM HE LEFT TO JOIN CELTIC

1011.	Regi Blinker	Chelsea
1012.	Michael Gray	Wolverhampton Wanderers
1013.	Paul Lambert	Middlesbrough
1014.	Ivan de la Pena	Hibernian
1015.	Alan Thompson	Roda JC Kerkrade
1016.	Chris Sutton	Espanyol
1017.	Didier Agathe	Aston Villa
1018.	Joos Valgaeren	Sunderland
1019.	Juninho Paulista	Sheffield Wednesday
1020.	Henri Camara	Borussia Dortmund

MORTEN WIEGHORST

1021. What nationality is Morten?

1022. In what year did Morten join Celtic?

1023. Name the Celtic Manager who brought Morten to Celtic Park.

1024. Can you recall from what Scottish Club Celtic signed Morten?

1025. To the nearest £50,000, how much did Celtic pay for Morten?

1026. How many goals did he score for Celtic during his time at Celtic Park - 15, 16 or 17?

1027. What Danish Club did he join when he left Celtic Park?

1028. Can you name his former team-mate who he joined at the Team in Q1027?

1029. With what Danish side did he begin his Professional career - Brondby IF, FC Copenhagen or Lyngby FC?

1030. What was his most productive season at Celtic Park for goals scored?

THE 1990s LEAGUE POSITIONS

ALL YOU HAVE TO DO HERE IS ASSOCIATE THE SEASON WITH CELTIC'S PLACING IN THE SCOTTISH PREMIER LEAGUE FOR THAT SEASON

1031.	Season 1989-1990	2nd
1032.	Season 1990-1991	4th
1033.	Season 1991-1992	4th
1034.	Season 1992-1993	2nd
1035.	Season 1993-1994	3rd
1036.	Season 1994-1995	1st
1037.	Season 1995-1996	5th
1038.	Season 1996-1997	3rd
1039.	Season 1997-1998	2nd
1040.	Season 1998-1999	3rd

THE UEFA CHAMPIONS LEAGUE

1041.   In what Group was Celtic for the 2001-2002 UEFA Champions League - D, E or F?

1042.   Name any 1 of Celtic's 3 opponents in the above Group.

1043.   Which 1 of the 3 Teams above inflicted Celtic's heaviest Group Stage defeat?

1044.   What Team did Celtic beat 5-0 on aggregate in the 2nd Qualifying Round of the 2003-2004 UEFA Champions League?

1045.   Can you recall the name of the Hungarian side that Celtic beat in the 3rd Qualifying Round to qualify for the 2003-2004 UEFA Champions League?

1046.   In what Group was Celtic for the 2003-2004 Champions League - A, B or C?

1047.   Name the German Team that was in Celtic's Group in Q1046.

1048.   Apart from the Team in Q1047, can you name either of the other 2 Teams that made up Celtic's Group?

1049.   In what Group was Celtic drawn for the 2004-2005 Champions League - F, G or H?

1050.   Name Celtic's 3 opponents in the Group in Q1049.

SUPER KENNY - 3

1051. In his early days at Celtic, Kenny Dalglish was farmed out to the Club's Nursery side. Name them.

1052. Kenny was given his first taste of first-team football at Celtic in a Benefit Match. Who were the opposition that day?

1053. How many goals did Kenny score in the 7-2 win over the Team in Q1052?

1054. In what season was he appointed Celtic Captain?

1055. Against what European country did Kenny Dalglish make his international debut for Scotland?

1056. Who appointed Kenny Dalglish the Captain of Scotland in 1978?

1057. Who replaced Kenny Dalglish as the Captain of Scotland after just 4 games as Captain?

1058. In what year was Kenny Dalglish voted the English Football Writers' Player of the Year?

1059. What legendary Brazilian player presented Kenny Dalglish with the English Football Writers' Player of the Year award in Q1058?

1060. In what year did Kenny Dalglish lead Newcastle United to the FA Cup Final

BOBBY LENNOX

1061. In what year did Bobby sign Professional forms with Celtic?

1062. What was his nickname at the Club?

1063. What other nickname was Bobby called by the fans?

1064. How many domestic League and Cup games did Bobby play for Celtic - 527, 537 or 547?

1065. How many domestic League and Cup goals did Bobby score for Celtic - 252, 262 or 272?

1066. How many full Scotland caps did he win?

1067. In what year was he awarded the MBE - 1981, 1982 or 1983?

1068. What North American Soccer League side did he join after he left Celtic?

1069. How many Scottish Championship Winners' medals did he win?

1070. How many Scottish FA Cup Winners' medals did he win?

SEASON 2003-2004
CHAMPIONS AGAIN

1071. By how many points did Celtic win the Scottish Premiership?

1072. What Team finished bottom of the league?

1073. How many points separated the Champions and the Team in Q1072 - 52, 62 or 72?

1074. Celtic recorded the highest league attendance of the season at Celtic Park. Who were the visitors?

1075. Celtic set the longest winning league sequence during the season. How many games did this entail - 15, 20 or 25?

1076. The highest aggregate score for a league game was 8 goals. Name either of the 2 Teams involved.

1077. Celtic recorded the biggest home win in the league of the season. What Team was beaten 6-0 at Celtic Park?

1078. Can you name the player who was Celtic's third-highest goalscorer in the league?

1079. Who did Celtic beat in the Scottish FA Cup Final?

1080. Who won the Scottish League Cup?

DIDIER AGATHE

1081.   From what Scottish Club did Celtic sign Didier?

1082.   For what French Club did Didier play prior to joining the Team in Q1081?

1083.   What Spanish Club was reportedly interested in signing Didier in November 2001?

1084.   In what city, sounding like a "French Apostle", was Didier born?

1085.   Was Didier born in 1975, 1976 or 1977?

1086.   In what season did Didier sign for Celtic?

1087.   Against what Team did he make his league debut for Celtic?

1088.   How many league goals did he score in Celtic's Treble Winning season 2000-2001?

1089.   How many appearances did he make for Celtic in his first season at Celtic Park - 25, 26 or 27?

1090.   In what season did he score his most goals for Celtic?

CELTIC'S ALL-TIME LEADING GOALSCORERS IN THE LEAGUE

ALL YOU HAVE TO DO HERE IS MATCH THE PLAYER WITH THE NUMBER OF LEAGUE GOALS HE SCORED FOR CELTIC

1091.	Jimmy Quinn	144
1092.	Adam McLean	167
1093.	Henrik Larsson	397
1094.	John Hughes	187
1095.	Steve Chalmers	115
1096.	Bobby Lennox	186
1097.	Jimmy McGrory	128
1098.	Sandy McMahon	159
1099.	Jimmy McMenemy	170
1100.	Patsy Gallacher	130

OLIVIER TEBILY

1101. At what French Club did Olivier begin his Professional career?

1102. What season was Olivier's only season at the Club in Q1101?

1103. What Yorkshire Club did Olivier sign for after leaving French football?

1104. In what year did Olivier sign for Celtic?

1105. What was his nickname at Celtic Park because it was said he caused so much panic in the Celtic defence?

1106. Name the Celtic Manager who brought Olivier Tebily to Celtic Park.

1107. When Olivier arrived at Celtic Park he was unveiled to the media alongside 2 other new signings. Name either of the other 2 new players.

1108. Against what Team did Olivier make his league debut for Celtic in a 5-0 away win?

1109. What country did Olivier represent at the African Cup of Nations during the 1999-2000 season?

1110. What English Club did he join after leaving Celtic?

THE SCOTTISH PREMIER LEAGUE

1111. In what year did Celtic last win the old Scottish First Division - 1972, 1973 or 1974?

1112. In what position did Celtic finish their last season in the old Scottish First Division - 2nd, 6th or 10th?

1113. In what position did Celtic finish their first season in the Scottish Premier League?

1114. How many times did Celtic win the Scottish Premier League before the Bank of Scotland sponsored it?

1115. In what season did the Bank of Scotland first sponsor the Scottish Premier League?

1116. How many times have Celtic won the Bank of Scotland Scottish Premier League?

1117. What was Celtic's lowest ever position in the Scottish Premier League before the Bank of Scotland sponsored it?

1118. Name any year in which Celtic finished in the position in Q1117.

1119. In what season did Celtic achieve the highest number of points in the Bank of Scotland Scottish Premier League?

1120. To the nearest 5, how many points did Celtic achieve in the season in Q1119?

ULRIK LAURSEN

1121. What nationality is Ulrik?

1122. In what season did Ulrik sign for Celtic?

1123. From what Scottish Club did Celtic sign Ulrik?

1124. How many seasons was he at the Club in Q1123?

1125. Who was the Manager of the Team in Q1123 that brought Ulrik into the Scottish Premier League?

1126. With what Danish Team did he begin his Professional career?

1127. In what season did he begin his Professional career with the Team in Q1126?

1128. How many goals did he score in his first season in Scottish football?

1129. Can you recall the newly promoted English Premier League Club that was interested in signing Ulrik in June 2004?

1130. What Swedish International joined Celtic on the same day that Ulrik arrived at Paradise?

MIXED BAG - 3

1131.   Prior to Barcelona's victory at Celtic Park on 14 September 2004, who were the last Team to record a victory over Celtic in Europe at Celtic Park?

1132.   When Celtic beat Rangers 1-0 on 29 August 2004, how many successive Old Firm victories had Celtic won?

1133.   Name the Celtic goalkeeper that let in 9 goals while playing for Scotland at Wembley in 1961.

1134.   Can you name the Celtic defender that made his debut for Scotland in a 9-3 loss to England at Wembley in 1961?

1135.   What English Premier League Club were reportedly interested in signing Bobo Balde in August 2004?

1136.   Prior to joining Celtic, how many UEFA Champions League appearances had Juninho made?

1137.   What was unfurled at Celtic Park on 8 August 2004?

1138.   To what 2 English Premier League Teams did Celtic lose on their 2004 USA Pre-season Tour?

1139.   What did Martin O'Neill "pick up" in London on 16 July 2004?

1140.   What Footballer's Agent in May 2004 labelled Martin O'Neill's offer to his player to come to Celtic Park for a trial an insult?

CHRIS SUTTON

1141.   In what season did Chris sign for Celtic?

1142.   Where in England was Chris born - Newcastle, Norwich or Nottingham?

1143.   From what Club did Celtic sign Chris?

1144.   Chris only scored 1 goal for the Team in Q1143. What Team did he score against?

1145.   Can you name the English Club that Chris played for prior to joining the Team in Q1143?

1146.   In what year did he join the Club in Q1145?

1147.   What is Chris's middle name - John, Michael or Roy?

1148.   Against what "United" did Chris make his Celtic league debut?

1149.   How many league goals did he score in Celtic's Treble Winning season 2000-2001?

1150.   At what English Club did Chris begin his Professional career?

MURDO MACLEOD

1151. At what Scottish Club did Murdo begin his Professional career?

1152. What season was Murdo's first with the Team in Q1151?

1153. How many goals did he score for the Team in Q1151 - 7, 8 or 9?

1154. In what year did Murdo join Celtic?

1155. What Celtic Manager brought Murdo to Paradise?

1156. How old was Murdo when he arrived at Celtic Park?

1157. How many league games did he play in his first season at Celtic Park - 23, 24 or 25?

1158. Against what Club did Murdo make his league debut for Celtic?

1159. In what season did Murdo score his most league goals for Celtic?

1160. What German Club did Murdo join when he left Celtic in June 1987?

SEASON 1985-1986

1161. Who did Celtic narrowly pip to the Scottish League Championship title?

1162. Celtic won the League Championship on goal difference, but how many points did they score - 50, 60 or 70?

1163. What Team won the Scottish FA Cup?

1164. How many league games did Celtic lose during the season?

1165. To the nearest 5, how many league goals did Celtic score?

1166. Who was Celtic's leading goalscorer in the league?

1167. What player made the most league appearances - Roy Aitken, Tommy Burns or Paul McStay?

1168. What was the score when Celtic met Rangers in the Old Firm game at Ibrox on 22 March 1986?

1169. Apart from the player in Q1166, can you name any other Celtic goalscorer in the game in Q1168?

1170. Can you recall in what position Rangers finished the league?

THE EARLY YEARS

1171.   What "Brother's" idea was it to form Celtic?

1172.   Can you name the "Order" in Glasgow of which the Brother in Q1171 was a member?

1173.   What Edinburgh-based Team gave the person in Q1171 the idea to form a similar Team in Glasgow?

1174.   In what part of Glasgow was Celtic's original home located - East, North or South?

1175.   In what year was the first meeting held to form Celtic?

1176.   What was the first name that was suggested for the new Football Club established by the person in Q1171?

1177.   How much was the yearly rent in the first season of the Club's history for Celtic's first ground situated close to where Celtic Park is located today?

1178.   How many Scottish League Championships did Celtic win before the outbreak of the First World War?

1179.   How many Scottish FA Cups did Celtic win before the outbreak of the First World War?

1180.   What colour were the shirts first adopted by Celtic?

DAVID HAY

1181.   In what year did David join Celtic?

1182.   From what Team's Boys' Club did Jock Stein bring David to Celtic Park?

1183.   In what year did David make his debut for Celtic?

1184.   How many International caps did he win with Scotland - 27, 37 or 47?

1185.   In what year did he leave Celtic Park on a transfer?

1186.   What English Team did David sign for after leaving Celtic?

1187.   In what year did David return to Celtic Park as the Manager?

1188.   Can you recall the season in which he guided Celtic to the Scottish League Championship?

1189.   With what Club did David achieve CIS Cup success in March 2004?

1190.   What Team did the Team in Q1189 beat in the Final?

PETER GRANT

1191. Where in Scotland was Peter born - Airdrie, Bellshill or Edinburgh?

1192. In what year did he make his debut for Celtic?

1193. Can you name the opposition in Q1192?

1194. What age was Peter when he made his debut for Celtic?

1195. What Celtic Team did Peter captain during the 1981-1982 season?

1196. How many league goals did Peter score for Celtic in their victorious 1985-1986 Championship winning season - 1, 3 or 5?

1197. What season was Peter's last at Celtic Park?

1198. In what season did Peter score his most league goals for Celtic?

1199. How many Scottish League Championships did he win with Celtic?

1200. To the nearest 25, how many league appearances did Peter make for Celtic?

EXPERT - IF YOU KNOW YOUR HISTORY - TRIVIA 1

1201. Can you name the Maltese Club, whose name begins and ends with the same letter, that Celtic met in the 1971-1972 European Cup?

1202. On how many occasions has Celtic won the "Domestic Treble" of Scottish Championship, Scottish FA Cup and Scottish League Cup?

1203. Following on from Q1202, name any 2 years in which Celtic won the "Domestic Treble"?

1204. Who in 1940 became the first Celtic player to manage the Club?

1205. By what affectionate "Sweets sounding gang" name was the Celtic Youth Team better known when Kenny Dalglish played for it?

1206. Against what team did Celtic secure their first away point(s) in a UEFA Champions League game?

1207. On how many occasions have Celtic won the "Domestic Double" of Scottish Championship and Scottish FA Cup?

1208. What was the score of the game when Celtic met Barcelona at Celtic Park on 14 September 2004 in the UEFA Champions League?

1209. How many times did Celtic win the Scottish Championship under Jimmy McGrory?

1210. Who played his last game for Celtic in the 1977 Scottish Cup Final win over Rangers before moving south of the Border?

EXPERT -
CELTIC IN THE EUROPEAN CUP -
UEFA CHAMPIONS LEAGUE

1211. What French Club was the first French side that Celtic met in the European Cup?

1212. Can you recall what season was the first season since 1966-1967 that Celtic did not compete in the European Cup?

1213. Name the 2 Belgian Clubs that Celtic have met in the competition.

1214. What British Club did Celtic beat in the 1970 Semi-Final?

1215. What Irish Club was the first Club that Celtic met in the 1st Qualifying Round of the UEFA Champions League?

1216. Name any 1 of the 4 Clubs that Celtic met in the 1971-1972 European Cup.

1217. Can you recall the Club that Celtic beat in the 3rd Qualifying Round to progress to the Group Stages of the 2001-2002 UEFA Champions League?

1218. What Team is the only Albanian Team that Celtic has played in the European Cup?

1219. Name all 3 Teams that made up Celtic's Group in the 2001-2002 UEFA Champions League.

1220. What Greek side put Celtic out of the 1974-1975 European Cup in the 1st Round?

EXPERT - SCOTTISH FA CUP
FINAL VICTORIES - 1

ALL YOU HAVE TO DO HERE IS ASSOCIATE THE TEAM WITH THE
YEAR CELTIC BEAT THEM IN THE SCOTTISH CUP FINAL

1221.	Rangers	1927
1222.	Hibernian	1969
1223.	Aberdeen	1995
1224.	East Fife	1925
1225.	Motherwell	1985
1226.	Dundee United	1914
1227.	Aberdeen	1951
1228.	Airdrieonians	1937
1229.	Dundee	1980
1230.	Rangers	1954

EXPERT - LISBON LIONS

1231. Can you recall the Lisbon Lion who scored a hat trick against Go Ahead Eagles Deventer in a 6-0 away win in the 1965-1966 European Cup Winners' Cup?

1232. What Scottish comedian narrates the documentary "Lord of the Wing", a tribute to Jimmy Johnstone?

1233. Who was Celtic's Left Half in the 1967 European Cup Final?

1234. Can you name the Lisbon Lion that represented Great Britain at the 1948 Olympics in London?

1235. Who scored a hat trick for Celtic in a 7-0 away win against Waterford in the 2nd Round of the 1970-71 European Cup?

1236. What Lisbon Lion was the last Celtic player to score in 3 consecutive Scottish FA Cup Finals for Celtic?

1237. Name the Lisbon Lion who scored twice in a 2-2 Old Firm draw at Ibrox on 6 May 1967 that enabled Celtic to retain the Scottish Championship that year.

1238. What was the surname of the Inter Milan goalkeeper in the 1967 European Cup Final?

1239. To the nearest 10, how many European appearances did Jimmy Johnstone make for Celtic?

1240. Who was Celtic's Inside Left in the 1967 European Cup Final?

EXPERT - CELTIC PLAYERS IN FRIENDLY INTERNATIONALS FOR SCOTLAND

1241. Name the Celtic striker who was a substitute for Scotland when they beat Norway 2-1 in Ullevaal Stadion, Oslo on 6 June 1974.

1242. Who was the Celtic midfielder that played against the USSR on 6 February 1991 at Ibrox Stadium?

1243. Can you name the Celtic striker that made his International debut for Scotland against East Germany at Hampden Park on 30 October 1974?

1244. Can you name the Celtic striker who was in the starting line-up for Scotland against Canada in Toronto on 19 June 1983?

1245. Name either of the 2 Celtic defenders that were in the starting line-up against Malta in Valetta on 1 June 1997.

1246. Can you name either of the 2 Celtic players that made their International debut for Scotland against Sweden at Hampden Park on 27 April 1977?

1247. How many Celtic players played for Scotland at the 1978 World Cup Finals in Argentina?

1248. Can you name the only Celtic player to have played against South Africa in Hong Kong in May 2002?

1249. Only 1 Celtic player played against England for Scotland in the SFA Centenary Match at Hampden Park on 14 March 1973. Name him.

1250. Can you name the Celtic defender who played for Scotland against Canada in the Empire Stadium, Vancouver on 12 June 1983?

EXPERT - AWAY GROUNDS

ALL YOU HAVE TO DO HERE IS MATCH CELTIC'S
OPPONENTS WITH THEIR HOME GROUND

1251.	Clyde	Strathclyde Homes Stadium
1252.	Hamilton Academical	Shielfield Park
1253.	Queen of the South	Cappielow Park
1254.	Ayr United	Broadwood Stadium
1255.	Arbroath	Glebe Park
1256.	Berwick Rangers	Station Park
1257.	Brechin City	Gayfield Park
1258.	Dumbarton	New Douglas Park
1259.	Forfar Athletic	Somerset Park
1260.	Greenock Morton	Palmerston Park

EXPERT - HENRIK LARSSON

1261.   Where in Sweden was Henrik born?

1262.   Can you name the Club where Henrik began his Professional career?

1263.   What was Henrik's first season with the Club in Q1262?

1264.   In what year did Henrik sign for Feyenoord?

1265.   How many goals did Henrik score for Sweden at the 2002 World Cup Finals?

1266.   Name any 3 seasons in which Henrik was the Scottish Premier League's top goal scorer.

1267.   Can you name any year in which Henrik won a Scottish FA Cup Winners' medal?

1268.   In what season did Henrik score 39 league goals for Celtic?

1269.   Against what Team did Henrik break his leg while playing for Celtic in the UEFA Cup on 21 October 1999?

1270.   In what season did Henrik win the Golden Boot Award for Europe's top goalscorer?

EXPERT - SEASON 1997-1998
10-IN-A-ROW BUSTERS

1271. Who did Celtic beat in the Scottish League Cup Final?

1272. What was the score of the game in Q1271?

1273. Where was the Final in Q1271 played?

1274. How many home games did Celtic win in the league?

1275. To the nearest 5, how many league goals did Celtic score at Celtic Park?

1276. How many goals did Henrik Larsson score in all competitions for Celtic?

1277. Apart from Henrik Larsson, can you name any other Celtic player who scored 10 league goals during the season?

1278. How many away games did Celtic win in the league?

1279. To the nearest 2, how many league goals did Celtic concede away from Celtic Park?

1280. Can you recall the Team that finished in 4th place?

EXPERT - IF YOU KNOW YOUR HISTORY - TRIVIA 2

1281. Can you name the Italian Club, whose name begins and ends with the same letter, that Celtic met in the 1969-1970 European Cup?

1282. Before managing Newcastle United, for what Team was Kenny Dalglish the European Scout?

1283. Who managed Celtic from 1897-1940?

1284. To what Club was Jimmy Johnstone farmed out for a while during his early years at Celtic Park?

1285. What was the first trophy that Kenny Dalglish won with Liverpool?

1286. Can you name the Lisbon Lion that began his football career as a 14-year-old with Queens Park?

1287. In what year did Celtic appear in their first Scottish FA Cup Final after World War II ended?

1288. How many times has Celtic successfully defended the Scottish League Cup?

1289. Who is the only man to have managed Celtic on 2 separate occasions?

1290. In what year did Brian McClair join Celtic from Motherwell?

EXPERT - THE 1930s
LEAGUE POSITIONS

ALL YOU HAVE TO DO HERE IS ASSOCIATE THE SEASON WITH CELTIC'S PLACING IN THE SCOTTISH FIRST DIVISION FOR THAT SEASON

1291.	Season 1929-1930	3rd
1292.	Season 1930-1931	1st
1293.	Season 1931-1932	2nd
1294.	Season 1932-1933	3rd
1295.	Season 1933-1934	1st
1296.	Season 1934-1935	3rd
1297.	Season 1935-1936	4th
1298.	Season 1936-1937	2nd
1299.	Season 1937-1938	2nd
1300.	Season 1938-1939	4th

EXPERT - TEAM NICKNAMES

ALL YOU HAVE TO DO HERE IS MATCH CELTIC'S
OPPONENTS WITH THEIR CLUB NICKNAME

1301.	Airdrie United	The Honest Men
1302.	Clyde	Wasps
1303.	Falkirk	Ton
1304.	Queen of the South	Loons
1305.	Alloa Athletic	Bairns
1306.	Ayr United	Diamonds
1307.	Arbroath	The Borderers
1308.	Berwick Rangers	Bully Wee
1309.	Forfar Athletic	Red Lichties
1310.	Greenock Morton	Doonhamers

EXPERT - CELTIC IN THE EUROPEAN CUP WINNERS' CUP

1311.   What Team is the only Austrian side that Celtic has met in the European Cup Winners' Cup?

1312.   In how many European Cup Winners' Cup competitions has Celtic played?

1313.   Name 4 seasons in which Celtic have played in the European Cup Winners' Cup.

1314.   What Team is the only Spanish side that Celtic has met in the European Cup Winners' Cup?

1315.   What Team were the first side to knock Celtic out of the European Cup Winners' Cup?

1316.   What was so unusual about the Team in Q1315's entry to the European Cup Winners' Cup that year?

1317.   How did Celtic help the winners of the 1972 European Cup Winners' Cup Final?

1318.   What Team is the only German side that Celtic has met in the European Cup Winners' Cup?

1319.   Can you name the Icelandic Team that Celtic beat in the 1st Round of the 1975-1976 competition?

1320.   Celtic has only ever played 1 Danish Team in the competition. Who did they beat in the 2nd Round of the 1965-1966 European Cup Winners' Cup?

EXPERT - CELTIC v. EASTERN EUROPEAN TEAMS IN EUROPE

ALL YOU HAVE TO DO HERE IS ASSOCIATE THE EASTERN EUROPEAN SIDE WITH THE YEAR AND THE EUROPEAN COMPETITION IN WHICH CELTIC PLAYED THEM

1321. Wisla Krakow (Pol)   European Cup Winners' Cup 1980-1981

1322. Croatia Zagreb (Cro)   European Cup 1988-1989

1323. Slovan Bratislava (Slo)   European Cup Winners' Cup 1980-1981

1324. Diosgyor Miskolc (Hun)   European Cup 1971-1972

1325. Politehnica Timisoara (Rom)   European Cup 1966-1967

1326. Vojvodinha Novi Sad (Yug)   European Cup 1968-1969

1327. Dinamo Kiev (Ukr)   European Cup Winners' Cup 1963-1964

1328. Red Star Belgrade (Yug)   European Cup 1967-1968

1329. Ujpest Budapest (Yug)   UEFA Cup 1976-1977

1330. Kispest-Honved Budapest (Hun) European Cup Winners' Cup 1963-1964

EXPERT - THE "OLD FIRM"

1331. Who scored a hat trick for Celtic in their 3-2 Scottish FA Cup Final victory over Rangers at Hampden Park in 1904?

1332. In what 1980 Cup Final did Rangers beat Celtic 3-1?

1333. Can you name the player that played for Celtic in 1901-02 and Rangers in 1907-09?

1334. Can you name the Celtic goalkeeper who died after fracturing his skull during an Old Firm game on 5 September 1931?

1335. What is the score in Scottish FA Cup Final wins when Celtic has met Rangers in the Final?

1336. Who famously scored a hat trick for Celtic in their 7-1 win over Rangers in the 1958 Scottish League Cup Final?

1337. Following on from Q1336, name any other Celtic goalscorer in the Final.

1338. Celtic appeared in 7 consecutive Scottish FA Cup Finals from 1969 to 1975. In which of these years did they meet Rangers in the Final?

1339. Name the Celtic player that scored a hat trick against Rangers in the 1973 Scottish League Cup Semi-Final against Rangers.

1340. Celtic's first ever game was a friendly against Rangers. What was the score of the game?

EXPERT - SEASON 1999-2000

1341.   Who did Celtic beat in the Scottish League Cup Final?

1342.   What was the score of the game in Q1341?

1343.   How many home games did Celtic lose in the league?

1344.   To the nearest 5, how many league goals did Celtic score at Celtic Park?

1345.   How many goals did Henrik Larsson score in the league for Celtic?

1346.   Can you name the Celtic player who scored 9 league goals, 1 CIS goal and 1 goal in Europe during the season?

1347.   How many away games did Celtic win in the league?

1348.   To the nearest 5, how many league goals did Celtic score away from Celtic Park?

1349.   Can you recall the Team that finished in 5th place?

1350.   Apart from the Old Firm, what Team had the best defensive record in the league?

EXPERT - OPPOSITION

1351.   Can you name the Eastern European Club, whose name begins and ends with the same letter, that Celtic met in the 1976-1977 UEFA Cup?

1352.   Name the only Team from Luxembourg that Celtic have played against in the UEFA Cup.

1353.   Who were Celtic's first ever opponents in a Scottish League Cup Final?

1354.   What Team is the only Romanian side that Celtic have met in the European Cup Winners' Cup?

1355.   From what Brazilian Club did Middlesbrough sign Juninho?

1356.   What French Club put Celtic out of the UEFA Cup in 2000-2001?

1357.   For what English Team was Pat Bonner playing in the 1978 FA Youth Cup Final when he was spotted by Jock Stein?

1358.   What Spanish Club put Celtic out of the UEFA Cup in 1964-1965?

1359.   Name 5 of the 7 Teams that Celtic played in the 2002-2003 UEFA Cup competition.

1360.   What Swiss Club put Celtic out of the UEFA Cup in 1991-1992?

EXPERT - IF YOU KNOW YOUR
HISTORY - PLAYERS

1361. Can you name the Surinam-born former Celtic striker whose name begins and ends with the same letter, e.g. Sean Peters.

1362. Name the Celtic player who was voted Scottish Football's Young Player of the Year in 2004.

1363. Name the Celtic player who was Europe's leading goalscorer in season 1915-1916.

1364. Can you name the 3 Celtic players who have been the top or joint-top goalscorer in Scotland on more than 1 occasion?

1365. What is Kenny Dalglish's middle name?

1366. Name the Celtic player who was voted Scottish Football's Young Player of the Year in 1981.

1367. What former Celtic player managed the Club between 1983 and 1987?

1368. What former Celtic player won a UEFA Champions League Winners' medal in 1997?

1369. When Typhoo Tea introduced Football Cards with their boxes of tea in 1967-1968, can you name either of the 2 Celtic players that were included in the first 20 numbered cards?

1370. Name the Celtic player who was Europe's leading goal scorer in seasons 1926-1927 and 1935-1936.

EXPERT - CHAMPIONS
OF EUROPE

1371. Can you name the Celtic defender that gave away the penalty in the 1967 Final?

1372. From what country was the referee for the 1967 Final?

1373. Name the player who scored Inter Milan's penalty in the 1967 Final?

1374. What was the name of the Inter Milan Manager in the 1967 Final?

1375. Whose shot across the face of the goal did Steve Chalmers redirect into the net to give Celtic victory in the 1967 Final?

1376. What Swiss side did Celtic beat in the First Round of the 1966-1967 European Cup?

1377. What Team were the only side to beat Celtic during their 1966-1967 European Cup Winning run?

1378. Who scored a last-minute goal against the Team in Q1377 at Celtic Park to give Celtic a 2-1 aggregate win over them?

1379. Who were the French Champions that Celtic beat in Round 2 of the 1966-1967 European Cup?

1380. Celtic beat the Team in Q1379 by the same score home and away. What was the total aggregate score of the 2 games?

EXPERT - SEASON 2000-2001
TREBLE WINNERS

1381. Who did Celtic beat in the Scottish FA Cup Final?

1382. What was the score of the game in Q1381?

1383. How many home games did Celtic win in the league?

1384. To the nearest 5, how many league goals did Celtic score at Celtic Park?

1385. How many goals did Henrik Larsson score in the league for Celtic?

1386. Can you name the Celtic player who scored 8 goals in all competitions - 7 league goals and 1 goal in Europe - during the season?

1387. How many away games did Celtic win in the league?

1388. To the nearest 5, how many league goals did Celtic score away from Celtic Park?

1389. Can you recall the Team that finished in 6th place?

1390. What Team had the second-best defensive record in the league behind Celtic?

EXPERT - SEASON 2004 - 2005

1391. Name the first team that Celtic played at home in the league.

1392. Can you recall the team Celtic recorded their first league away victory against?

1393. What team were the first team to beat Celtic during the season?

1394. Name the team Celtic beat 8-1 in the Scottish League Cup.

1395. Who ended Celtic's proud unbeaten home league record when they won 3-2 at Celtic Park on 27th October?

1396. Against what team did Celtic record their first win in the 2004-2005 UEFA Champions League?

1397. What was result of the second Old Firm meeting of the season?

1398. Who were the first team to take points off Celtic in the league?

1399. Following on from Q1398, what was the score of the game?

1400. Who scored Celtic's first goal of the season?

EXPERT - CELTIC IN THE FAIRS/UEFA CUP

1401.   Up to and including the 2003-2004 competition, how many consecutive appearances had Celtic made in the UEFA Cup?

1402.   What Team did Celtic meet in the 1983-1984 UEFA Cup and again 10 years later in the 1993-1994 UEFA Cup?

1403.   How many times has Celtic entered the UEFA Cup as a result of being knocked out of the UEFA Champions League?

1404.   Following on from Q1403, name any 3 seasons up to season 2003-2004 in which this took place.

1405.   Name the 2 Spanish Clubs that Celtic met in the 2003-2004 competition.

1406.   What Team were the first Team to put Celtic out of the Fairs Cup?

1407.   Can you name the German side that Celtic have met in two different UEFA Cup competitions, losing out on both occasions?

1408.   Apart from the Team in Q1407, can you name 2 other German sides that Celtic have played in the competition?

1409.   What Portuguese side were the first Team that Celtic beat over 2 legs in the competition?

1410.   Name the 2 French Teams that Celtic have played against in the UEFA Cup.

EXPERT - PAST PLAYERS

1411. Who is the only Celtic player to have played for 4 different Clubs that have all been European Champions?

1412. Can you name the Celtic goalkeeper from the 1930s that represented Canada, Scotland and the USA at full International level?

1413. Name the Celtic player that scored for the Scottish League against the Italian League in November 1962.

1414. Can you name the English-born player who was the first Englishman to win an English FA Cup Winners' medal and a Scottish FA Cup Winners' medal?

1415. What Celtic player holds the record as being the only player to score a hat-trick in both the Scottish FA Cup Final and the Scottish League Cup Final?

1416. Can you name the first Celtic player to have scored in successive Scottish FA Cup Finals?

1417. Can you name the former Celtic player who has a statue erected in his memory in Prague?

1418. Only 2 Celtic players are in the top 10 of all-time leading goalscorers in Scottish Football's Top Division. Name them.

1419. Who was the first Scottish-born Celtic player to be capped by the Republic of Ireland?

1420. What legendary Celtic player scored twice from a corner in the same game against Falkirk?

EXPERT - THE 1950s
LEAGUE POSITIONS

*ALL YOU HAVE TO DO HERE IS ASSOCIATE THE SEASON
WITH CELTIC'S PLACING IN THE SCOTTISH FIRST DIVISION
FOR THAT SEASON*

1421.	Season 1949-1950	8th
1422.	Season 1950-1951	3rd
1423.	Season 1951-1952	5th
1424.	Season 1952-1953	6th
1425.	Season 1953-1954	7th
1426.	Season 1954-1955	5th
1427.	Season 1955-1956	2nd
1428.	Season 1956-1957	1st
1429.	Season 1957-1958	9th
1430.	Season 1958-1959	5th

EXPERT - IF YOU KNOW
YOUR HISTORY - TRIVIA 3

1431. How many goals did Jimmy Johnstone score in Europe during Celtic's 1966-1967 European Cup winning season?

1432. What club did Henri Camara sign for when he left Celtic?

1433. Who did Kenny Dalglish replace as the Manager of Newcastle United?

1434. How many total Championships did Kenny Dalglish win both as a player and as a Manager?

1435. In 1971 what team stopped Celtic from winning their 6th successive Scottish League Cup?

1436. To the nearest 10, how many league goals did Kenny Dalglish score in total for both Celtic and Liverpool?

1437. Name the Celtic player who was voted Scottish Football's Young Player of the Year in 2001.

1438. Name the Celtic player who was placed joint 3rd for Europe's leading goal scorer in season 1982-1983 with 29 league goals.

1439. What is the highest number of consecutive seasons that Celtic have played in the European Cup?

1440. How many league goals did Henrik Larsson score during the season in which he won the Golden Boot Award as Europe's leading goal scorer?

EXPERT - SEASON 2001-2002

1441. What was the score in the Scottish FA Cup Final?

1442. How many home games did Celtic win in the league?

1443. To the nearest 5, how many league goals did Celtic score?

1444. How many goals did Henrik Larsson score in the league for Celtic?

1445. Apart from Henrik Larsson and John Hartson, can you name the Celtic player who scored 10 goals in all competitions during the season?

1446. How many away games did Celtic fail to win in the league?

1447. To the nearest 5, how many league goals did Celtic score away from Celtic Park?

1448. Can you recall the Team that finished in 3rd place?

1449. What Team finished highest - Aberdeen, Dundee United or Hearts?

1450. Who put Celtic out of the UEFA Cup?

EXPERT - JOCK STEIN -
THE LION KING

1451.   With what Club did Jock start his playing career?

1452.   In what year did he captain Celtic to a League and Cup "Double"?

1453.   In what year was he appointed the Manager of Dunfermline Athletic?

1454.   What was the first trophy he won as a Manager?

1455.   In what year was he appointed the Manager of Hibernian?

1456.   How many times did Celtic win the Scottish League Cup under his management?

1457.   In what year did he first guide Celtic to Scottish League Cup success under his management?

1458.   In what year was he badly injured in a car crash?

1459.   Who took charge of Celtic for a while following the incident in Q1458?

1460.   Apart from the Scottish FA Cup and the Scottish League Cup, what other Cup did Celtic win 4 times when he was their Manager?

EXPERT - JIMMY JOHNSTONE

1461. Where in Scotland was Jimmy born?

1462. What English League Club attempted to sign Jimmy as a 13-year-old before Celtic offered him a job as a ball boy?

1463. What famous American actor, who starred in "The Godfather", told BBC viewers in October 2000 that he had named his Scottish Terrier dog after Jimmy Johnstone?

1464. Against what Club did he make his debut for Celtic?

1465. To the nearest 10, how many Scottish League appearances did he make?

1466. How many caps did Jimmy win for the Scottish League Team?

1467. How many Scottish League Cups did Jimmy win with Celtic?

1468. What ranking for Europe's Best Player was Jimmy nominated in a France-Football poll of Sports Writers in 1967?

1469. Can you recall the "planet sounding" Team that Jimmy was selected in 1967 to play against?

1470. How many European goals did Jimmy score during his Celtic career?

EXPERT - SUPER KENNY

1471. How many appearances did Kenny Dalglish make for Liverpool?

1472. How many goals did Kenny score for Liverpool - 162, 172 or 182?

1473. How many caps did he win for Scotland?

1474. How many goals did he score for Scotland - 30, 35 or 40?

1475. Kenny is the joint-holder of the record for scoring the most goals for Scotland. With whom does he share this record?

1476. What was the first trophy won by Kenny Dalglish as a Manager?

1477. In what year did he guide Blackburn Rovers to FA Premiership success?

1478. Can you recall the year in which Kenny won the European Super Cup with Liverpool?

1479. On how many occasions did he win the League Cup with Liverpool?

1480. Name any 2 years he won a League Cup Winners' medal with Liverpool.

EXPERT - SCOTTISH FA CUP
FINAL VICTORIES - 2

*ALL YOU HAVE TO DO HERE IS ASSOCIATE THE TEAM WITH THE
SCORE CELTIC BEAT THEM BY IN THE SCOTTISH CUP FINAL*

1481.	Dunfermline 2004	3-0
1482.	Aidrieonians 1995	3-2
1483.	Rangers 1971 (Replay)	4-2
1484.	Hibernian 2001	1-0
1485.	Dundee United 1985	4-0
1486.	Dunfermline Athletic 1965	1-0
1487.	Rangers 1969	3-1
1488.	Motherwell 1931	2-1
1489.	Hibernian 1972	2-1
1490.	Rangers 1977	6-1

EXPERT - IF YOU KNOW YOUR HISTORY - TRIVIA 4

1491.   What was so unusual about the Celtic Team that drew 0-0 away to Kilmarnock in a league game on 19 November 1994?

1492.   Name the Celtic player who scored the last ever goal in a Scottish League v. League of Ireland game that was played at Celtic Park in September 1970.

1493.   Celtic came closest to being relegated from Scottish Football's Top Flight in season 1947-1948. In what position, their lowest ever, did they finish in the league?

1494.   What European Team were the visitors to Celtic Park when Celtic recorded their lowest ever attendance for a home game?

1495.   Remarkably, Celtic played 2 games on the same day in 1916. Can you name either opponent?

1496.   Apart from Rangers, what was the only other Team to have defeated Celtic in the league during their 1968-1969 Scottish Championship winning season?

1497.   Prior to their 2000-2001 Treble Winning season, when was the last season that Celtic won all 3 major trophies in Scotland?

1498.   In what 1973 Cup Final did Hibernian beat Celtic 5-3 after extra time?

1499.   In what year did Celtic last play a Scottish First Division game on Christmas Day or who were the opponents?

1500.   Name the only Celtic player to have played in a Scottish League v. Welsh League game that took place in Cardiff in September 1952.

ANSWERS

THE BOSS - MARTIN O'NEILL - 1

1. Distillery
2. Nottingham Forest
3. Manchester City
4. Norwich City (February 1981 - May 1981 & February 1982 - August 1983)
5. Grantham Town
6. Notts County
7. Wycombe Wanderers
8. Division 2
9. Nottingham Forest
10. Norwich City

SEASON 2000-2001 TREBLE WINNERS

11. 15 (Celtic 97 points to Rangers 82)
12. St Mirren
13. 67
14. Hibernian
15. St Mirren
16. 9
17. Rangers
18. Aberdeen & Kilmarnock
19. Lubo Moravcik (with 12 goals - 9 league & 3 Europe)
20. Kilmarnock

HENRIK LARSSON

21. 1997
22. Wim Jansen
23. Feyenoord
24. 4
25. The Scottish League Cup
26. 2001
27. Helsingborgs IF
28. 16 (in 35 games)
29. 5
30. 2

IF YOU KNOW YOUR HISTORY - PLAYERS 1

31.   Paul Lambert
32.   Roy Aitken, Tom Boyd, John Collins, Kenny Dalglish, Danny McGrain & Paul McStay
33.   Tommy Boyd (it was an own goal!)
34.   Neil Lennon
35.   1985
36.   Dariusz Dziekanowski
37.   Paul McStay (76 caps)
38.   Anton Rogan
39.   George Connelly
40.   Sporting Lisbon

CHAMPIONS OF EUROPE

41.   1967
42.   Inter Milan
43.   Celtic 2, Inter Milan 1
44.   Tommy Gemmell & Steve Chalmers
45.   Jock Stein
46.   Dukla Prague
47.   The National Stadium, Lisbon, Portugal
48.   The Lisbon Lions
49.   Ronnie Simpson
50.   Penalty

PAOLO DI CANIO

51.   1996
52.   AC Milan
53.   Lazio, Ternana, Napoli & Juventus
54.   37
55.   Sheffield Wednesday
56.   Paul Allcock
57.   West Ham United & Charlton Athletic
58.   Scottish Football Professional Player of the Year
59.   Manchester United (at Old Trafford)
60.   West Ham United (16 goals from 30 games in season 1999-2000)

SQUAD NUMBERS - 1

61.   Didier Agathe   17
62.   Bobby Petta   15
63.   Henri Camara   27

64.	Neil Lennon	18
65.	Joos Valgaeren	5
66.	Stephen Pearson	11
67.	Stanislav Varga	23
68.	Ulrik Laursen	16
69.	Jackie McNamara	4
70.	Juninho Paulista	7

IF YOU KNOW YOUR HISTORY - TRIVIA 1

71. BBC TV's Quizball Trophy
72. Liverpool (Semi-Final)
73. Inter Cardiff
74. Jock Stein
75. Michael Jordan (Jordan is Henrik's son)
76. Season 1997-1998
77. Middlesbrough
78. Sir Alex Ferguson
79. 2 & 7
80. Tommy Boyd

LUBOMIR MORAVCIK

81. 1998-1999
82. Czechoslovakia (now Slovakia)
83. 1990 (in Italy)
84. MSV Duisburg
85. Bundesliga (German League)
86. Slovakian Player of the Year
87. Bastia & AS St-Etienne
88. 9
89. Rangers (in the Scottish FA Cup Final)
90. Dr Josef Venglos (former Celtic Manager & Czechoslovakian Coach)

MOVING ON - 1

91.	Henrik Larsson	Barcelona
92.	Regi Blinker	RBC Roosendahl
93.	Colin Healy	Coventry City
94.	Tommy Johnson	Everton
95.	Magnus Hedman	Ancona
96.	Mark Viduka	Leeds United
97.	Mark Burchill	Ipswich Town
98.	Bobby Petta	Fulham

| 99. | Alan Stubbs | Everton |
| 100. | Steve Guppy | Leicester City |

SEASON 1993-1994

101. 4th
102. Aberdeen (2nd) & Motherwell (3rd)
103. 8 (Rangers 58 to Celtic's 50)
104. Dundee
105. Rangers
106. Celtic 2, Rangers 4
107. Mark Hateley (of Rangers with 22 goals)
108. Pat McGinlay
109. 10
110. John Collins & Charlie Nicholas (both players scored 8 goals)

SUPER KENNY

111. 6
112. 1970, 1971, 1972, 1973, 1974 & 1977
113. 2 (1970 & 1975)
114. 1975
115. 1977
116. 7
117. 1978-1979, 1979-1980, 1981-1982, 1982-1983, 1983-1984, 1985-1986 & 1987-1988
118. 3
119. 1978, 1981 & 1984
120. Blackburn Rovers

LIAM BRADY

121. Billy McNeill
122. 1991
123. Chippy
124. Arsenal
125. The English Professional Footballers' Association Player of the Year
126. Juventus
127. Ascoli, Inter Milan & Sampdoria
128. 3rd (in 1991-1992 & 1992-1993)
129. Brighton & Hove Albion
130. Lou Macari

SCOTTISH CUP FINAL VICTORIES

131.	Hibernian	2001
132.	Aberdeen	1967
133.	Rangers	1989
134.	Hibernian	1972
135.	Dundee United	1988
136.	Airdrieoneans	1975
137.	Dunfermline Athletic	2004
138.	Rangers	1971
139.	Airdrieoneans	1995
140.	Dunfermline Athletic	1965

ROY AITKEN

141.   1975-1976
142.   Scottish Division 1 (the Premier League started the following season)
143.   17
144.   Aberdeen (in a 1-0 away win)
145.   Newcastle United
146.   St Mirren
147.   Irvine (24 November 1958)
148.   1982-1983 (6 goals)
149.   15 (1975-1990)
150.   Aberdeen

THE "OLD FIRM"

151.   2002 (Celtic lost 3-2)
152.   They all signed for Rangers (at the time SFA regulations required all players

        competing in the game to be registered to a single SFA Member Club)
153.   Beattie, Conway, Crerand, Kennedy & Tully
154.   Joe Conway
155.   Jackie McNamara
156.   Alfie Conn Jnr (Rangers 1968-1974 & Celtic 1977-1979)
157.   Andy Lynch (he scored a penalty)
158.   14
159.   Jimmy Quinn
160.   Riots took place in the Replay after the first game ended 2-2

LISBON LIONS - 1

161.   Steve Chalmers
162.   Billy McNeill

163. The Flea
164. European Cup, the Scottish Championship, Scottish FA Cup & the Scottish League Cup
165. Bobby Lennox
166. Tommy Gemmell
167. 200
168. Ronnie Simpson (Goalkeeper)
169. Billy McNeill (1978-1983 & 1987-1991)
170. 92

PAT BONNER

171. 1978
172. Jock Stein
173. Packie
174. Irish
175. 23
176. Romania
177. Gordon Marshall
178. 80
179. 4
180. 3

THE SCOTTISH PROFESSIONAL FOOTBALLERS' ASSOCIATION PLAYER OF THE YEAR

181. Henrik Larsson   1999
182. Paul McStay   1988
183. Paolo di Canio   1997
184. Chris Sutton   2004
185. Davie Provan   1980
186. Brian McClair   1987
187. Charlie Nicholas   1983
188. Paul Elliott   1991
189. Mark Viduka   2000
190. Jackie McNamara   1998

THE HISTORY OF CELTIC - 1

191. 1888
192. Rangers
193. 4 (winners in 1892)
194. 1893
195. They won the Scottish "Double"

196. The Empire Exhibition Trophy
197. Hibernian
198. To celebrate the crowning of Queen Elizabeth II
199. The Scottish League Cup
200. 7-1

PIERRE VAN HOOIJDONK

201. NEC Breda
202. 1995
203. £1,200,000
204. Hearts (in a 1-1 draw at Celtic Park on 11 January 1995)
205. 26
206. Nottingham Forest
207. SBV Vitesse Arnhem
208. Benfica
209. Feyenoord
210. Fenebahce (Turkey - in a 1-0 win over Sparta Prague)

I PLAYED FOR BOTH

211.	Alfie Conn Jnr	Rangers 1968-74 & Celtic 1977-79
212.	David Taylor	Rangers 1906-11 & Celtic 1918-19 (Guest Player)
213.	Robert Campbell	Celtic 1905-06 & Rangers 1906-14
214.	Davie McLean	Celtic 1907-09 & Rangers 1918-19
215.	Hugh Shaw	Rangers 1905-06 & Celtic 1906-07
216.	Willie Kivlichan	Rangers 1905-07 & Celtic 1907-11
217.	Tom Sinclair	Rangers 1904-06 & Celtic 1906-07
218.	Scott Duncan	Rangers 1913-18 & Celtic 1918-19 (Guest Player)
219.	Maurice Johnston	Celtic 1984-87 & Rangers 1989-92
220.	James Young	Celtic 1917-18 & Rangers 1917-18

CELTIC v. EASTERN EUROPEAN TEAMS IN EUROPE

221.	1.FC Kosice (Slo)	UEFA Cup 1996-1997
222.	Partizan Belgrade (Yug)	European Cup Winners' Cup 1989-1990
223.	Dinamo Batumi (Geo)	European Cup Winners' Cup 1995-1996
224.	FK Suduva (Lit)	UEFA Cup 2002-2003
225.	FK Teplice (Cze)	UEFA Cup 2003-2004
226.	Dukla Prague (Cze)	European Cup 1966-1967

227.	Partizani Tirana (Alb)	European Cup 1979-1980
228.	Croatia Zagreb (Cro)	UEFA Champions League 1998-1999
229.	FC Kaunas (Lit)	UEFA Champions League 2003-2004
230.	MTK Hungaria (Hun)	UEFA Champions League 2003-2004

JUNINHO

231. Middlesbrough
232. Henrik Larsson's No. 7 shirt
233. Glasgow Rangers (29 August 2004)
234. 1997 FIFA Confederations Cup
235. Germany (as a substitute)
236. Sao Paulo FC
237. Vasco da Gama
238. Atletico de Madrid
239. Flamengo, Middlesbrough & Vasco da Gama
240. 1995

THE BOSS - MARTIN O'NEILL - 2

241. Nottingham Forest
242. 1980 (he was left out of the Team in the 1979 Final)
243. 64
244. Manchester United
245. Norwich City (player 1981 & 1982-1983 and Manager 1995)
246. Kenny Dalglish
247. 2000
248. Celtic 6, Rangers 2
249. 2000-2001
250. Chesterfield

SEASON 1996-1997

251. 5 (Rangers 80 points to Celtic's 75)
252. Raith Rovers
253. Rangers
254. Dundee United
255. Dunfermline Athletic 2, Rangers 5; & Rangers 4, Hibernian 3
256. Kilmarnock
257. Jorge Cadete
258. 25
259. Pierre van Hooijdonk (with 14)
260. Dundee United (3rd)

TOMMY BOYD

261. Motherwell
262. 1983-1984
263. Chelsea (the FA Premier League began in 1992-1993)
264. Ian Porterfield (scored in Sunderland's 1-0 win over Leeds United in 1973)
265. 1992 (6 February 1992)
266. Tony Cascarino
267. Liam Brady
268. Airdrieonians (8 February 1992 in a 2-0 home win)
269. Real Mallorca
270. 42 (season 1992-1993)

CELTIC PLAYERS IN THE BRITISH HOME INTERNATIONAL CHAMPIONSHIPS

271. Kenny Dalglish (Northern Ireland won 2-1)
272. Billy Bremner
273. Jimmy Johnstone
274. Andy Gray
275. Davy Provan
276. Roy Aitken
277. Kenny Dalglish, David Hay & Danny McGrain
278. Danny McGrain
279. Alistair Robert Hunter
280. Charlie Nicholas

FORMER CLUBS - 1

281. Stephen Pearson   Motherwell
282. Jonathan Gould   Coventry City
283. Ulrik Laursen   Hibernian
284. Henrik Larsson   Feyenoord
285. Mohammed Sylla   St Johnstone
286. Lubomir Moravcik   Duisburg
287. Dmitri Kharine   Chelsea
288. Bobo Balde   Toulouse
289. Stephane Mahe   Paris Saint-Germain
290. Daniel da Cruz Carvalho Dani   Atletico de Madrid

PAUL McSTAY

291. 1981
292. Jimmy McStay & Willie McStay

293.   1990
294.   Roy Aitken
295.   2
296.   1985-1986 & 1987-1988
297.   None (he was a one-Club player)
298.   76
299.   1986 (Mexico) & 1990 (Italy)
300.   1997

IF YOU KNOW YOUR HISTORY - PLAYERS 2

301.   Peter Grant
302.   Manchester United
303.   Mark McGhee & Charlie Nicholas
304.   Paul & Willie McStay
305.   Jackie McNamara
306.   1998-1999
307.   Paul Lambert
308.   John Hughes (versus FC Basel in the ECWC - the first by any Scottish player)
309.   England
310.   Kenny Dalglish (with Liverpool)

THE 1970s LEAGUE POSITIONS

311.   Season 1969-1970   1st
312.   Season 1970-1971   1st
313.   Season 1971-1972   1st
314.   Season 1972-1973   1st
315.   Season 1973-1974   1st
316.   Season 1974-1975   3rd
317.   Season 1975-1976   2nd
318.   Season 1976-1977   1st
319.   Season 1977-1978   5th
320.   Season 1978-1979   1st

JACKIE McNAMARA

321.   1995-1996
322.   Glasgow (24 October 1973)
323.   Dunfermline Athletic
324.   £600,000
325.   1991-1992
326.   Tommy Burns

327.	Falkirk (in a 1-0 away win on 4 October 1995)
328.	26
329.	3
330.	6 (Tommy Burns, Wim Jansen, Dr Josef Venglos, John Barnes, Kenny Dalglish & Martin O'Neill)

IF YOU KNOW YOUR HISTORY - TRIVIA 2

331.	Shamrock Rovers (1st Round)
332.	Alan McInally (Aston Villa, Bayern Munich & Celtic)
333.	1993, 1994, 1996 & 1997
334.	Atletico de Madrid
335.	Rapid Vienna (Season 1984-1985)
336.	Glasgow Rangers
337.	Sean Fallon
338.	Alan Thompson
339.	Dunfermline Athletic (1961-1962)
340.	Tommy Boyd

CELTIC v. FRENCH AND ITALIAN TEAMS IN EUROPE

341.	Olympique Lyon	UEFA Cup 1999-2000
342.	Bordeaux	UEFA Cup 2000-2001
343.	Paris Saint-Germain	European Cup Winners' Cup 1995-1996
344.	FC Nantes	European Cup 1966-1967
345.	Inter Milan	European Cup 1966-1967
346.	St-Etienne	European Cup 1968-1969
347.	AC Milan	European Cup 1968-1969
348.	AC Fiorentina	European Cup 1969-1970
349.	Juventus	European Cup 1981-1982
350.	FC Lyon	UEFA Champions League 2003-2004

JIMMY JOHNSTONE

351.	1961
352.	Connolly (James Connolly Johnstone)
353.	Jinky
354.	Flying
355.	Glasgow Rangers
356.	23
357.	9
358.	4
359.	1975

360.   David Hay

SCOTLAND'S LEADING GOAL SCORER - 1

361.	Henrik Larsson	2004
362.	George McCluskey	1982
363.	Steve Chalmers	1967
364.	Tommy Coyne	1991
365.	Charlie Nicholas	1983
366.	Jorge Cadete	1997
367.	Mark McGhee	1989 (Joint)
368.	Pierre Van Hooijdonk	1996
369.	Brian McClair	1987
370.	Henrik Larsson	2001

CELTIC PLAYERS IN WORLD CUP
GAMES FOR SCOTLAND

371.   Paul McStay (played against Brazil & Costa Rica - sub against Sweden)
372.   George Connelly & Alistair Hunter
373.   David Hay
374.   Roy Aitken & Paul McStay
375.   Jackie McNamara
376.   Kenny Dalglish, David Hay & Danny McGrain
377.   Roy Aitken
378.   Paul McStay
379.   Tommy Boyd & Tosh McKinlay
380.   Craig Burley (Chelsea) & Paul Lambert (Borussia Dortmund)

CHARLIE NICHOLAS

381.   1980-1981
382.   Kilmarnock (as a sub in a 3-0 win at Kilmarnock on 16 August 1980)
383.   18
384.   Cowcaddens (30 December 1961)
385.   16
386.   1983
387.   £650,000
388.   Aberdeen
389.   8 (1980-1983 & 1990-1995)
390.   1982-1983

JOCK STEIN - THE LION KING

391. Miner
392. 1951
393. Dunfermline Athletic
394. Hibernian
395. 1965
396. 10 (1966-1974 & 1977)
397. Leeds United
398. Scotland
399. 1985
400. Wales

NATIONALITIES - 1

401. Henrik Larsson   Swedish
402. Liam Miller   Irish
403. Paolo di Canio   Italian
404. John Hartson   Welsh
405. Bobo Balde   French
406. Ramon Vega   Swiss
407. Joos Valgaeren   Belgian
408. Colin Healy   Irish
409. Lubomir Moravcik   Czechoslovakian
410. Morten Wieghorst   Danish

JOHN COLLINS

411. Hibernian
412. 1985-1986
413. 1990 (13 July)
414. 1
415. 1991-1992 or 1995-1996 (11 goals in each season)
416. AS Monaco
417. 1996
418. Everton
419. £2,500,000
420. Fulham

SEASON 1997-1998 10-IN-A-ROW BUSTERS

421. Wim Jansen
422. 2 (Celtic 74 points to Rangers' 72)
423. Hibernian
424. 34

425.	St Johnstone
426.	8
427.	Hearts 5, Kilmarnock 3; & Motherwell 6, Hibernian 2
428.	Marco Negri (Rangers - 32 goals)
429.	Hearts (beat Rangers 2-1)
430.	Celtic

LISBON LIONS - 2

431.	Jimmy Johnstone
432.	Stevie Chalmers (in Celtic's 5-1 win in 1966)
433.	Willie Wallace
434.	Billy McNeill
435.	Jim Craig
436.	2
437.	Bobby Lennox
438.	Ronnie Simpson
439.	48
440.	Tommy Gemmell, Bobby Murdoch, Ronnie Simpson & Willie Wallace (at Windsor Park on 21 October 1967 versus Northern Ireland in a Home International & European Championship - Group 8 qualifying game)

SUPER KENNY - 2

441.	Joe Fagan
442.	1985-1986
443.	1991
444.	1999
445.	£440,000
446.	Bob Paisley
447.	3
448.	2
449.	1979 & 1983
450.	1983

FORMER CLUBS - 2

451.	Eyal Berkovic	West Ham United
452.	Craig Burley	Chelsea
453.	Javier Sanchez Broto	Livingston
454.	Paolo di Canio	AC Milan
455.	Neil Lennon	Leicester City
456.	Stanislav Varga	Sunderland
457.	Ramon Vega	Tottenham Hotspur

458.	Tommy Johnson	Aston Villa
459.	Alan Stubbs	Bolton Wanderers
460.	John Hartson	Wimbledon

RUNNERS-UP

461.	Season 1986-1987	Rangers
462.	Season 1984-1985	Aberdeen
463.	Season 1983-1984	Aberdeen
464.	Season 1982-1983	Dundee United
465.	Season 1979-1980	Aberdeen
466.	Season 1975-1976	Rangers
467.	Season 1954-1955	Aberdeen
468.	Season 1938-1939	Rangers
469.	Season 1934-1935	Rangers
470.	Season 1930-1931	Rangers

DANNY McGRAIN

471.	1970
472.	Morton (in a 2-0 home win on 29 August 1970)
473.	Sean Fallon (ironically the game was played at Ibrox)
474.	His skull
475.	6
476.	1977
477.	650 (including 10 as a sub)
478.	4
479.	1982 (came on as a sub against the USSR - he missed the 1978 Finals with a broken ankle)
480.	The MBE

CELTIC v. GERMAN & BELGIAN TEAMS IN EUROPE

481.	Borussia Dortmund	UEFA Cup 1987-1988
482.	Anderlecht	UEFA Champions League 2003-2004
483.	FC Cologne	UEFA Cup 1992-1993
484.	Borussia Dortmund	UEFA Cup 1992-1993
485.	SV Hamburg	UEFA Cup 1996-1997
486.	KAA Gent	European Cup Winners' Cup 1984-1985
487.	FSV Zwickau	European Cup Winners' Cup 1975-1976
488.	Stuttgart	UEFA Cup 2002-2003
489.	Werder Bremen	European Cup 1988-1989

TEAM NICKNAMES - 1

491.	Hibernian	The Hibees
492.	Kilmarnock	Killie
493.	Hearts	The Jambos
494.	Dundee	The Dee
495.	Aberdeen	The Dons
496.	Livingston	The Livi Lions
497.	Raith Rovers	Rovers
498.	Brechin City	The City
499.	Dumbarton	The Sons
500.	Stirling Albion	Albion

STILIAN PETROV

511.
501.   Sofia (Montana)
502.   1999-2000
503.   CSKA Sofia
504.   1997-1998
505.   7
506.   Dundee United (in a 2-1 away defeat on 15 August 1999)
507.   26
508.   3 (John Barnes, Kenny Dalglish & Martin O'Neill)
509.   Inter Milan
510.   2002-2003 (12 goals)

SEASON 1999-2000

511.   21
512.   Aberdeen
513.   St Johnstone
514.   11 goals
515.   Motherwelll 5, Aberdeen 6
516.   Mark Viduka (24 goals)
517.   Rangers (beat Aberdeen 4-0)
518.   Mark Burchill (with 11 goals)
519.   Aberdeen
520.   Celtic

CELTIC'S ALL-TIME LEADING GOAL SCORERS

521.	Bobby Lennox	273
522.	Sandy McMahon	177

523.	Jimmy Quinn	217
524.	Jimmy McGrory	470
525.	Kenny Dalglish	167
526.	Stevie Chalmers	232
527.	Patsy Gallacher	192
528.	Henrik Larsson	235
529.	John Hughes	188
530.	Jimmy McMenemy	168

DIANBOBO BALDE

531. 2001-2002 (21 July 2001)
532. Marseilles
533. Guinea
534. Toulouse
535. He was signed on a free transfer
536. AS Cannes
537. Celtic (he scored an own goal in Celtic's 2-2 away draw with Hibernian on 19 September 2004)
538. 22
539. Marseilles
540. 6

MIXED BAG - 1

541. Umbro
542. Liverpool (ECWC 1965-66, UEFA Cup 1977-78 & UEFA Cup 2002-03)
543. Kenny Dalglish (102 caps)
544. Craig Bellamy (From Newcastle United)
545. Pierre van Hooijdonk
546. The Scottish League Cup in 2001
547. The Pools Panel
548. Goalkeeper
549. Paul McStay
550. Carling

CELTIC v. PORTUGUESE AND DUTCH TEAMS IN EUROPE

551.	Sporting Lisbon	UEFA Cup 1983-1984
552.	Sporting Lisbon	UEFA Cup 1993-1994
553.	Go Ahead Eagles Deventer	European Cup Winners' Cup 1965-1966
554.	Boavista	UEFA Cup 2002-2003

555.	Porto	UEFA Cup 2002-2003
556.	Benfica	European Cup 1969-1970
557.	Ajax Amsterdam	European Cup 1970-1971
558.	Ajax Amsterdam	European Cup 1982-1983
559.	Ajax Amsterdam	UEFA Champions League 2001-2002
560.	Porto	UEFA Champions League 2001-2002

JOHN HARTSON

561. 2001-2002
562. Swansea (5 April 1975)
563. Coventry City
564. Luton Town (1993-1995)
565. Arsenal
566. Kilmarnock (as a sub in a 1-0 away win on 4 August 2001)
567. 31
568. 19
569. Northern Ireland (in a 2-2 draw)
570. West Ham United & Wimbledon

THE SCOTTISH FOOTBALL WRITERS' PLAYER OF THE YEAR

571.	Danny McGrain	1977
572.	Billy McNeill	1965
573.	Henrik Larsson	2001
574.	Brian McClair	1987
575.	Craig Burley	1998
576.	Paul Lambert	2002
577.	Bobby Murdoch	1969
578.	Charlie Nicholas	1983
579.	Ronnie Simpson	1967
580.	Paul McStay	1988

THE HISTORY OF CELTIC - 2

581. Inter Milan (in a penalty shoot-out)
582. 1974
583. Ajax Amsterdam
584. 1979 (beating Rangers 4-2 at Celtic Park in their final game)
585. David Hay
586. Dundee United (2-1 in 1985)

587.	5-0
588.	The Scottish "Double" of League Championship & FA Cup
589.	Joe Miller
590.	Liam Brady (1991-1993)

JORGE CADETE
591.	Portuguese
592.	Brescia Calcio
593.	1996
594.	Tommy Burns
595.	Celta Vigo
596.	Bradford City
597.	Benfica
598.	Partick Thistle (February-March)
599.	Mozambique
600.	Paolo di Canio & Pierre van Hooijdonk

SCOTTISH CUP FINAL LOSSES
601.	Rangers	1973
602.	Clyde	1955
603.	Dunfermline Athletic	1961
604.	Rangers	2002
605.	Aberdeen	1990
606.	Rangers	1966
607.	Aberdeen	1984
608.	Heart of Midlothian	1956
609.	Aberdeen	1970
610.	Rangers	1999

THE BOSS - MARTIN O'NEILL - 3
611.	Fulham
612.	Northern Ireland (The 1982 World Cup Finals in Spain)
613.	A knee injury
614.	Shepshed Charterhouse
615.	1991 & 1992
616.	Norwich City
617.	Mark McGhee
618.	1995
619.	Crystal Palace
620.	The League Cup (with Leicester City in 1997 - Coca-Cola Cup)

PAUL LAMBERT

621. 1997-1998 (7 November 1997)
622. Glasgow (7 August 1969)
623. Borussia Dortmund
624. £2,000,000
625. Motherwell
626. 1993
627. Rangers (in a 1-0 loss at Ibrox on 8 November 1997)
628. 26
629. 2
630. St Mirren

SEASON 2001-2002

631. 18 (Celtic 103 points to Rangers' 85)
632. St Johnstone
633. 82
634. Dundee United
635. 14
636. Dundee United, 1 Rangers 6; Dunfermline 5, Motherwell 2; & Hibernian 3, Aberdeen 4
637. John Hartson
638. Rangers
639. Ayr United (Rangers beat them 4-0)
640. Dunfermline Athletic

PLAYER NICKNAMES

641. Jimmy Johnstone   Jinky
642. Pat Bonner   Packie
643. Bobby Lennox   Fizz Bomb
644. Henrik Larsson   The Magnificent 7
645. Billy McNeill   Caesar
646. Brian McClair   Choccy
647. Alan McInally   Rambo
648. John Hughes   Yogi
649. Johannes Edvaldsson Shuggie
650. Dariusz Dziekanokski Jackie

JOHAN MJALLBY

651. Swedish
652. 1998
653. AIK Solna (Sweden)

654. 9
655. Rangers (in a 5-1 home win on 21 November 1998)
656. Bolton Wanderers
657. 4
658. Levante UD
659. 2000 (European Championships in Belgium & Holland)
660. Michael Owen (Liverpool)

MOVING ON - 2

661.	Liam Miller	Manchester United
662.	Stephane Mahe	Hearts
663.	Eyal Berkovic	Blackburn Rovers
664.	Vidar Riseth	Munchen 1860
665.	Stephane Bonnes	Partick Thistle
666.	Olivier Tebily	Birmingham City
667.	Pat Crerand	Manchester United
668.	Jonathan Gould	Preston North End
669.	Malky Mackay	Norwich City
670.	Mark McGhee	Newcastle United

NATIONALITIES - 2

671.	Regi Blinker	Dutch
672.	Tommy Johnson	English
673.	Vidar Riseth	Norwegian
674.	Johan Mjallby	Swedish
675.	Mark Viduka	Australian
676.	Bobby Petta	Dutch
677.	Magnus Hedman	Swedish
678.	Steve Guppy	English
679.	Jonathan Gould	Scottish
680.	Eyal Berkovic	Israeli

RONNIE SIMPSON

681. Queens' Park
682. 14
683. Hibernian
684. Rangers
685. Third Lanark
686. Newcastle United
687. Arsenal (1952) & Manchester City (1954)
688. Hibernian (October 1960)

689. Jock Stein
690. It was his 39 birthday

IF YOU KNOW YOUR HISTORY - PLAYERS 3
691. Henrik Larsson
692. Ally McCoist (Rangers)
693. 1985-1986
694. Malcolm MacDonald
695. Mark McGhee (then at Hamburg - versus England at Wembley on 26 May 1984)
696. Paul McStay (came on as a substitute for Gordon Strachan at Wembley on 26 May 1984 in a 1-1 draw)
697. Mo Johnston (Celtic 1984-1987 & Rangers 1989-1992)
698. Pat Crerand (when Manchester United beat Benfica in the 1968 Final)
699. Tommy Coyne
700. Brian McClair (with Celtic in 1985 & with Manchester United in 1994)

IF YOU KNOW YOUR HISTORY - TRIVIA 3
701. They both won competitions in Europe in 1967 (Celtic won the European Cup & Sandy won the Eurovision Song Contest with "Puppet on a String")
702. Tony Cascarino (Aston Villa, Celtic & Marseilles)
703. Jock Stein in 1965
704. ntl:
705. Ronnie Simpson (aged 36 years and 186 days v. England at Wembley in a 3-2 win for Scotland. This was England's first defeat since winning the World Cup in 1966)
706. Liverpool
707. Chris Sutton
708. Bertie Peacock
709. 145
710. Season 2003-2004 (Celtic beat Rangers 1-0 on 7 March 2004)

NEIL LENNON
711. 2000
712. Aberdeen (in a 6-0 home win on 16 December 2000)
713. Leicester City
714. £5,750,000
715. Manchester City
716. Crewe Alexandria
717. Dario Grady

718. 1994
719. The League Cup (in 1997 & 2000)
720. Cyprus

CELTIC v. SCANDINAVIAN TEAMS IN EUROPE

721.	AGF Aarhus (Den)	UEFA Cup 1983-1984
722.	HJK Helsinki (Fin)	UEFA Cup 2000-2001
723.	B1903 Copenhagen (Den)	European Cup 1971-1972
724.	AGF Aarhus (Den)	European Cup Winners' Cup 1965-1966
725.	KPV Kokkola (Fin)	European Cup 1970-1971
726.	Valur Reykjavik (Ice)	European Cup Winners' Cup 1975-1976
727.	Rosenborg Trondheim (Nor)	European Cup 1972-1973
728.	TPS Turku (Fin)	European Cup 1973-1974
729.	Vejle BK (Den)	European Cup 1973-1974
730.	Rosenborg (Nor)	UEFA Champions League 2001-2002

SCOTTISH FA CUP FINALS - 1

731. 2
732. Aberdeen (1984) & Rangers (1980)
733. 1 (Rangers 1980)
734. Aberdeen
735. 9-8
736. Queen's Park (5-1 in 1892)
737. Third Lanark (2-1 in 1889)
738. 3 (1965, 1967 & 1969)
739. Rangers (3-2 in 2002)
740. 34

MIXED BAG - 2

741. Marcio Amoroso
742. Frederic Kanoute
743. Lennart Johansson
744. David Hay
745. Hearts
746. Chris Sutton & Didier Agathe
747. 76
748. FC Porto
749. Germany
750. Stephen Pearson (£350,000 from Motherwell)

IN THE HOT SEAT

751.	Liam Brady	1991-1993
752.	Jozef Venglos	1998-1999
753.	Jock Stein	1965-1978
754.	Billy McNeill	1978-1983
755.	Lou Macari	1993-1994
756.	Wim Jansen	1997-1998
757.	Kenny Dalglish	2000
758.	Jimmy McGrory	1945-1965
759.	Tommy Burns	1994-1997
760.	John Barnes	1999-2000

THE 1980s LEAGUE POSITIONS

761.	Season 1979-1980	2nd
762.	Season 1980-1981	1st
763.	Season 1981-1982	1st
764.	Season 1982-1983	2nd
765.	Season 1983-1984	2nd
766.	Season 1984-1985	2nd
767.	Season 1985-1986	1st
768.	Season 1986-1987	2nd
769.	Season 1987-1988	1st
770.	Season 1988-1989	3rd

TOMMY BURNS

771.	1975
772.	Dundee (as a sub in a 2-1 defeat at Celtic Park on 19 April 1975)
773.	16
774.	9
775.	1981-1982 & 1983-1984
776.	Kilmarnock
777.	The match was abandoned
778.	1994
779.	Falkirk
780.	Reading

SQUAD NUMBERS - 2

781.	Alan Thompson	8
782.	Stilian Petrov	19
783.	Mohammed Sylla	3
784.	Chris Sutton	9

785.	Paul Lambert	14
786.	John Hartson	10
787.	Dianbobo Balde	6
788.	Robert Douglas	20
789.	David Fernandez	12
790.	Ross Wallace	33

THE WORLD CLUB CHAMPIONSHIP

791. 1967
792. Inter Milan (who they beat 2-1 in the 1967 European Cup Final)
793. Jock Stein
794. Racing Club
795. Argentina
796. Celtic 1 Racing Club 0
797. Racing Club 2 Celtic 1
798. Racing Club 1 Celtic 0
799. He was hit with a missile during the warm-up
800. Montevideo (the 2nd leg prior to this game was played in Buenos Aires)

BILLY McNEILL

801. 1958
802. 23
803. Clyde
804. Aberdeen
805. Aston Villa & Manchester City
806. An MBE
807. 29
808. Jock Stein
809. Dunfermline Athletic (Celtic won 3-2)
810. 790

SEASON 2002-2003

811. None (Celtic lost out to Rangers on goal difference)
812. Motherwell
813. Rangers
814. 8
815. Dundee
816. Aberdeen
817. John Hartson (18 goals - Larsson 28)
818. Sutton 4 (Hartson 3 & Petrov 2)
819. Kilmarnock (4th)

820.   Rangers 2 Celtic 1

SCOTTISH LEAGUE CUP FINAL LOSSES

821.	Raith Rovers	1995
822.	Rangers	2003
823.	Aberdeen	1977
824.	Rangers	1991
825.	Hibernian	1973
826.	Rangers	2003
827.	Dundee	1974
828.	Rangers	1987
829.	Partick Thistle	1972
830.	Rangers	1965

VIDAR RISETH

831.   Norwegian
832.   1998
833.   Dr Josef Venglos
834.   Hearts (in a 1-1 draw at Celtic Park on 26 September 1998)
835.   Aberdeen (Celtic won 2-0)
836.   TSC Munich 1860
837.   Rosenborg Trondheim
838.   1998-1999 (scored 3 goals)
839.   LASK Linz
840.   Jeunesse Esch

WIM JANSEN

841.   Tommy Burns
842.   Jonathan Gould
843.   1997-1998
844.   St Johnstone
845.   Henrik Larsson and Harold Brattbakk
846.   The Coca-Cola Cup (in November 1997)
847.   Paul Lambert (from Borussia Dortmund)
848.   Tommy Boyd, Jackie McNamara & Alan Stubbs (Cadete, di Canio & van Hooijdonk had all left over the summer and Paul McStay retired through injury)
849.   Marc Rieper
850.   Feyenoord (when they beat Celtic in the 1970 Final)

MOVING ON - 3

851.	Stephen Crainey	Southampton
852.	Charlie Nicholas	Arsenal
853.	Ramon Vega	Watford
854.	Didier Agathe	Hibernian
855.	David Fernandez	Livingston
856.	Paolo di Canio	Sheffield Wednesday
857.	Kenny Dalglish	Liverpool
858.	Craig Burley	Derby County
859.	Lou Macari	Manchester United
860.	Pierre van Hooijdonk	NAC Breda

NATIONALITIES - 3

861.	Stilian Petrov	Bulgarian
862.	Stephane Mahe	French
863.	Dmitri Kharine	Russian
864.	Neil Lennon	Irish
865.	Alan Thompson	English
866.	Pat Bonner	Irish
867.	Billy McNeill	Scottish
868.	Juninho Paulista	Brazilian
869.	Mohammed Sylla	Ivory Coast
870.	Pierre van Hooijdonk	Dutch

EYAL BERKOVIC

871.	Maccabi Haifa
872.	Southampton
873.	1996
874.	1999-2000
875.	Aberdeen (1 August 1999 in a 5-0 away win)
876.	West Ham United
877.	John Hartson
878.	Blackburn Rovers
879.	Manchester City
880.	Portsmouth

CELTIC v. UK AND IRISH TEAMS IN EUROPE

881.	Nottingham Forest	UEFA Cup 1983-1984
882.	Inter Cardiff	UEFA Cup 1997-1998
883.	Cwmbran Town	UEFA Cup 1999-2000
884.	Liverpool	UEFA Cup 1965-1966

885.	Liverpool	UEFA Cup 2002-2003
886.	Leeds United	European Cup 1969-1970
887.	Waterford United	European Cup 1970-1971
888.	Dundalk	European Cup 1979-1980
889.	Shamrock Rovers	European Cup 1986-1987
890.	St Patrick's Athletic	UEFA Champions League 1998-1999

SCOTLAND'S LEADING GOAL SCORER - 2

891.	Henrik Larsson	2002
892.	Brian McClair	1984
893.	Kenny Dalglish	1976
894.	Joe McBride	1966
895.	Mark Viduka	2000
896.	Frank McGarvey	1981
897.	Charlie Nicholas	1989 (Joint)
898.	Harry Hood	1971
899.	Bobby Lennox	1968
900.	Henrik Larsson	1999

BRIAN McCLAIR

901.	Airdrie (8 December 1963)
902.	Aston Villa
903.	Motherwell
904.	The Scottish League Cup
905.	1
906.	99
907.	£850,000
908.	24
909.	4
910.	Nottingham Forest

TEAM NICKNAMES - 2

911.	Motherwell	The Well
912.	Dunfermline Athletic	The East Enders
913.	St Johnstone	The Saints
914.	Dundee United	The Terrors
915.	St Mirren	The Buddies
916.	Partick Thistle	The Jags
917.	Rangers	Gers
918.	Inverness Caledonian Thistle	Caley Thistle
919.	Hamilton Academical	The Accies

920.	Ross County	The County

SCOTTISH LEAGUE CUP FINAL VICTORIES

921.	Kilmarnock	2001
922.	Hibernian	1975
923.	Dundee United	1998
924.	Aberdeen	2000
925.	Rangers	1983
926.	Hibernian	1969
927.	Dundee	1968
928.	Rangers	1966
929.	St Johnstone	1970
930.	Partick Thistle	1957

TOMMY JOHNSON

931.	Notts County
932.	1996
933.	Aston Villa
934.	Derby County
935.	£2,400,000
936.	Tommy Burns
937.	The Scottish League Cup Final (in a 2-0 win over Aberdeen)
938.	Raith Rovers (in a 1-1 away draw on 5 April 1997)
939.	Everton
940.	Sheffield Wednesday

IF YOU KNOW YOUR HISTORY - PLAYERS 4

941.	David Moyes (Everton Manager)
942.	Paul McStay (aged 19 when Aberdeen beat Celtic 2-1 in 1984)
943.	Brian McClair
944.	George Connelly, David Hay, Jimmy Johnstone & Harry Hood
945.	4
946.	Charlie Tully
947.	Tommy Burns
948.	Ally McCoist (1984 Scottish League Cup Final - Celtic lost 3-2 after extra time)
949.	Lou Macari
950.	Henrik Larsson (v. Kilmarnock in the 2001 League Cup Final)

IF YOU KNOW YOUR HISTORY - TRIVIA 4

951.	Jock Stein

952. Season 1997-1998
953. Paul McStay
954. Croatia Zagreb
955. 1987
956. Stilian Petrov (Lubo Moravcik was a Czech)
957. Kenny Dalglish
958. CR Smith
959. Olivier Tebily
960. Liam Brady, Joe Jordan & Frank Connor

ALAN THOMPSON

961. 2000-2001 (1 September 2000)
962. Newcastle (22 December 1973)
963. Aston Villa
964. £2,750,000
965. Bolton Wanderers
966. £4,750,000
967. Newcastle United (the English Premier League only began in season 1992-1993)
968. 1991-1992
969. Hibernian (in a 3-0 win at Celtic Park on 9 September 2000)
970. Kilmarnock (on 14 August - he scored the winner against Rangers on 29 August)

HENRI CAMARA

971. Wolverhampton Wanderers
972. Senegalese
973. Dakar (10 May 1977)
974. CS Sedan-Ardennes
975. Neuchatel Xamax FC & Grasshopper-Club Zurich
976. Strasbourg
977. The African Cup of Nations
978. Dundee (he scored 2 in a 3-0 win on 11 September 2004)
979. 30
980. 7

LISBON LIONS - 3

981. Willie Wallace
982. Gordon Banks
983. Bobby Murdoch
984. Steve Chalmers (3 January 1966)

985.   Ronnie Simpson
986.   Tommy Gemmell
987.   Bobby Lennox
988.   Jimmy Johnstone
989.   Steve Chalmers
990.   Willie Wallace

THE BOSS - MARTIN O'NEILL - 4
991.   Kilrea (1 March 1952)
992.   1971
993.   USSR
994.   The League Cup (1978)
995.   1978
996.   Hamburg (1980)
997.   285 (21 as a sub)
998.   1984
999.   Finland (Northern Ireland won 2-1)
1000. 1993

ALAN STUBBS
1001. Bolton Wanderers
1002. 1990-1991
1003. 1996
1004. Tommy Burns
1005. £3,500,000
1006. 2 (1998 & 2001)
1007. 1
1008. 2001 (13 July on a free transfer)
1009. Everton
1010. Richard Gough

FORMER CLUBS - 3
1011.	Regi Blinker	Sheffield Wednesday
1012.	Michael Gray	Sunderland
1013.	Paul Lambert	Borussia Dortmund
1014.	Ivan de la Pena	Espanyol
1015.	Alan Thompson	Aston Villa
1016.	Chris Sutton	Chelsea
1017.	Didier Agathe	Hibernian
1018.	Joos Valgaeren	Roda JC Kerkrade
1019.	Juninho Paulista	Middlesbrough

1020.   Henri Camara   Wolverhampton Wanderers

MORTEN WIEGHORST

1021.   Danish
1022.   1995
1023.   Tommy Burns
1024.   Dundee
1025.   £600,000
1026.   16
1027.   Brondby IF
1028.   Marc Rieper
1029.   Lyngby FC
1030.   1997-1998 (4 goals)

THE 1990s LEAGUE POSITIONS

1031.	Season 1989-1990	5th
1032.	Season 1990-1991	3rd
1033.	Season 1991-1992	3rd
1034.	Season 1992-1993	3rd
1035.	Season 1993-1994	4th
1036.	Season 1994-1995	4th
1037.	Season 1995-1996	2nd
1038.	Season 1996-1997	2nd
1039.	Season 1997-1998	1st
1040.	Season 1998-1999	2nd

THE UEFA CHAMPIONS LEAGUE

1041.   Group E
1042.   FC Porto, Juventus & Rosenborg
1043.   Porto (3-0)
1044.   Kaunas
1045.   MTK Hungary
1046.   Group A
1047.   Bayern Munich
1048.   Anderlecht & Olympique Lyonnais
1049.   Group F
1050.   AC Milan, Barcelona & Shakhtar Donetsk

SUPER KENNY - 3

1051.   Cumbernauld United
1052.   Kilmarnock

1053. 6
1054. 1975-1976
1055. Belgium
1056. Jock Stein
1057. Archie Gemmill
1058. 1983
1059. Pele
1060. 1998

BOBBY LENNOX

1061. 1961
1062. Buzz Bomb
1063. Lemon (because he made the defenders look like suckers)
1064. 537
1065. 272
1066. 10
1067. 1981
1068. Houston Hurricanes
1069. 9
1070. 8

SEASON 2003-2004 CHAMPIONS AGAIN

1071. 17 (Celtic 98 points to Rangers 81)
1072. Partick Thistle
1073. 72
1074. Dunfermline Athletic
1075. 25
1076. Motherwell 5 Dundee 3
1077. Hibernian
1078. Alan Thompson (11 goals - Larsson 30 & Sutton 19 - Hartson 8)
1079. Dunfermline Athletic (3-1)
1080. Livingston

DIDIER AGATHE

1081. Hibernian
1082. Montpellier
1083. Valencia
1084. Saint Pierre
1085. 1975 (16 August)
1086. 2000-2001 (1 September)
1087. St Mirren (in a 2-0 home win on 14 October 2000)

1088.   3
1089.   27
1090.   2003-2004 (5 goals)

CELTIC'S ALL-TIME LEADING GOALSCORERS IN THE LEAGUE

1091.	Jimmy Quinn	187
1092.	Adam McLean	128
1093.	Henrik Larsson	170
1094.	John Hughes	115
1095.	Steve Chalmers	159
1096.	Bobby Lennox	167
1097.	Jimmy McGrory	397
1098.	Sandy McMahon	130
1099.	Jimmy McMenemy	144
1100.	Patsy Gallacher	186

OLIVIER TEBILY

1101.   Chateauroux
1102.   1997-1998
1103.   Sheffield United
1104.   1999
1105.   Bombscare
1106.   John Barnes
1107.   Eyal Berkovich & Bobby Petta
1108.   Aberdeen (1 August 1999)
1109.   Ivory Coast
1110.   Birmingham City

THE SCOTTISH PREMIER LEAGUE

1111.   1973
1112.   10th (1974-1975)
1113.   2nd (1975-1976)
1114.   6
1115.   2000-2001
1116.   4
1117.   5th
1118.   1978, 1982 & 1990
1119.   2001-2002
1120.   103

ULRIK LAURSEN

1121.   Danish
1122.   2002-2003
1123.   Hibernian
1124.   2 (2000-2002)
1125.   Alex McLeish
1126.   Odense BK
1127.   1993-1994
1128.   2 (with Hibernian in 2000-2001)
1129.   Norwich City
1130.   Magnus Hedman

MIXED BAG - 3

1131.   Ajax Amsterdam (August 2001)
1132.   7
1133.   Frank Haffey (Scotland lost 9-3)
1134.   Billy McNeill
1135.   Newcastle United
1136.   None
1137.   The Championship Flag
1138.   Chelsea & Liverpool
1139.   A CBE from the Queen
1140.   Rivaldo

CHRIS SUTTON

1141.   2000-2001
1142.   Nottingham (10 March 1973)
1143.   Chelsea
1144.   Manchester United
1145.   Blackburn Rovers
1146.   1994
1147.   Roy
1148.   Dundee United (in a 2-1 away win on 30 July 2000)
1149.   11
1150.   Norwich City

MURDO MACLEOD

1151.   Dumbarton
1152.   1975-1976
1153.   7
1154.   1978

1155. Jock Stein
1156. 20 (born on 24 September 1958)
1157. 23
1158. Motherwell (in a 2-1 away loss on 4 November 1978)
1159. 1982-1983 (11 goals)
1160. Borussia Dortmund

SEASON 1985-1986

1161. Hearts
1162. 50
1163. Aberdeen (beat Hearts 3-0 in the Final at Hampden Park)
1164. 6
1165. 67
1166. Brian McClair (with 22 goals)
1167. Roy Aitken with 36 (Tommy Burns & Paul McStay made 34 each)
1168. 4-4
1169. Tommy Burns, Mo Johnson & Murdo MacLeod
1170. 5th

THE EARLY YEARS

1171. Brother Wilfrid
1172. The Marist Order
1173. Edinburgh Hibernian
1174. East End
1175. 1887 (formed in 1888)
1176. Celtic
1177. £50
1178. 11
1179. 9
1180. The Green & White Hoops

DAVID HAY

1181. 1965
1182. St Mirren Boys' Club
1183. 1967
1184. 27
1185. 1974
1186. Chelsea
1187. 1983
1188. 1985-1986
1189. Livingston

1190.   Hibernian (2-0)

PETER GRANT
1191.   Bellshill
1192.   1984 (21 April)
1193.   Rangers (Celtic lost 1-0 at Ibrox)
1194.   18 (born on 30 August 1965)
1195.   The Celtic Boys' Club Team
1196.   1
1197.   1996-1997 (he spent 15 years at the Club)
1198.   1984-1985 (4 goals)
1199.   2 (1986 & 1988)
1200.   338

EXPERT - IF YOU KNOW YOUR HISTORY - TRIVIA 1
1201.   Sliema Wanderers (2nd Round)
1202.   3
1203.   1967, 1969 & 2001
1204.   Jimmy McStay
1205.   The Quality Street Gang
1206.   Barcelona
1207.   13
1208.   Celtic 1 Barcelona 3
1209.   1 (1953-1954)
1210.   Kenny Dalglish (he joined Liverpool)

EXPERT - CELTIC IN THE EUROPEAN CUP - UEFA CHAMPIONS LEAGUE
1211.   FC Nantes (2nd Round in 1966-1967)
1212.   Season 1975-1976 (Rangers won the 1974-1975 Scottish Championship)
1213.   KAA Gent (1984-1985) & Anderlecht (2003-2004)
1214.   Leeds United
1215.   St Patrick's Athletic (1998-1999)
1216.   B1903 Copenhagen, Inter Milan, Sliema Wanderers & Ujpest Budapest
1217.   Ajax Amsterdam
1218.   Partazani Tirana (1979-1980)
1219.   Juventus, Porto & Rosenborg
1220.   Olympiakos Piraeus

EXPERT - SCOTTISH FA CUP FINAL VICTORIES - 1

1221.	Rangers	1980
1222.	Hibernian	1914
1223.	Aberdeen	1954
1224.	East Fife	1927
1225.	Motherwell	1951
1226.	Dundee United	1985
1227.	Aberdeen	1937
1228.	Airdrieonians	1995
1229.	Dundee	1925
1230.	Rangers	1969

EXPERT - LISBON LIONS

1231. Bobby Lennox
1232. Billy Connolly
1233. John Clark
1234. Ronnie Simpson (Goalkeeper)
1235. Willie Wallace
1236. Bobby Lennox (1969 v. Rangers, 1970 v. Aberdeen & 1971 v. Rangers)
1237. Jimmy Johnstone
1238. Sarti
1239. 67
1240. Bertie Auld

EXPERT - CELTIC PLAYERS IN FRIENDLY INTERNATIONALS FOR SCOTLAND

1241. Kenny Dalglish
1242. Paul McStay
1243. John Kelly (Dixie) Deans
1244. Charlie Nicholas
1245. Tommy Boyd & Tosh McKinlay
1246. Ronnie Glavin & Joseph Craig (came on as a second-half substitute)
1247. None (Kenny Dalglish moved to Liverpool in 1977)
1248. Rob Douglas
1249. Kenny Dalglish
1250. Tommy Burns

EXPERT - AWAY GROUNDS

1251.	Clyde	Broadwood Stadium
1252.	Hamilton Academical	New Douglas Park

1253.	Queen of the South	Palmerston Park
1254.	Ayr United	Somerset Park
1255.	Arbroath	Gayfield Park
1256.	Berwick Rangers	Shielfield Park
1257.	Brechin City	Glebe Park
1258.	Dumbarton	Strathclyde Homes Stadium
1259.	Forfar Athletic	Station Park
1260.	Greenock Morton	Cappielow Park

EXPERT - HENRIK LARSSON

1261. Helsingborg (20 September 1971)
1262. Högaborg
1263. 1988-1989
1264. 1993
1265. 3
1266. 1998-1999, 2000-2001, 2001-2002, 2002-2003 & 2003-2004
1267. 2001 & 2004
1268. 2001-2002 & 2003-2004
1269. Olympique Lyon
1270. 2000-2001

EXPERT - SEASON 1997-1998 10-IN-A-ROW BUSTERS

1271. Dundee United
1272. Celtic 3 Dundee United 0
1273. Ibrox Stadium
1274. 12
1275. 41 (conceded 9)
1276. 19 (16 league & 3 CIS)
1277. Craig Burley & Simon Donnelly
1278. 10
1279. 15 (scored 23)
1280. Kilmarnock

EXPERT - IF YOU KNOW YOUR HISTORY - TRIVIA 2

1281. AC Fiorentina (Quarter-Final)
1282. Glasgow Rangers
1283. Willie Maley
1284. Celtic Blantyre
1285. European Super Cup (1977)
1286. Ronnie Simpson (Goalkeeper)
1287. 1951 (Celtic 2 Motherwell 1)

1288.   6 (Winners in 1957-1958, 1996-1970 & 2000-2001)
1289.   Billy McNeill (1978-1983 & 1987-1991)
1290.   1983

EXPERT - THE 1930s LEAGUE POSITIONS

1291.   Season 1929-1930   4th
1292.   Season 1930-1931   2nd
1293.   Season 1931-1932   3rd
1294.   Season 1932-1933   4th
1295.   Season 1933-1934   3rd
1296.   Season 1934-1935   2nd
1297.   Season 1935-1936   1st
1298.   Season 1936-1937   3rd
1299.   Season 1937-1938   1st
1300.   Season 1938-1939   2nd

EXPERT - TEAM NICKNAMES

1301.   Airdrie United   Diamonds
1302.   Clyde   Bully Wee
1303.   Falkirk   Bairns
1304.   Queen of the South   Doonhamers
1305.   Alloa Athletic   Wasps
1306.   Ayr United   The Honest Men
1307.   Arbroath   Red Lichties
1308.   Berwick Rangers   The Borderers
1309.   Forfar Athletic   Loons
1310.   Greenock Morton   Ton

EXPERT - CELTIC IN THE EUROPEAN CUP WINNERS' CUP

1311.   Rapid Vienna (2nd Round in 1984-1985)
1312.   8
1313.   1963-64, 1965-66, 1975-76, 1980-81, 1984-85, 1985-86, 1989-90 & 1995-96
1314.   Atletico de Madrid (1st Round in 1985-1986)
1315.   MTK Budapest (Semi-Final in 1963-1964)
1316.   No domestic Cup Final was played in Hungary in 1963 and they qualified by finishing second to Ferencváros in their league
1317.   Celtic won the Scottish "Double" in 1971 allowing Rangers, the Team they beat in the Scottish Cup Final, to participate in the 1971-1972 ECWC
1318.   FSV Zwickau (Quarter-Final in 1975-1976)

1319.   Valur Reykjavik
1320.   AGF Aarhus

EXPERT - CELTIC v. EASTERN EUROPEAN TEAMS IN EUROPE

1321.	Wisla Krakow (Pol)	UEFA Cup 1976-1977
1322.	Croatia Zagreb (Cro)	European Cup Winners' Cup 1963-1964
1323.	Slovan Bratislava (Slo)	European Cup Winners' Cup 1963-1964
1324.	Diosgyor Miskolc (Hun)	European Cup Winners' Cup 1980-1981
1325.	Politehnica Timisoara (Rom)	European Cup Winners' Cup 1980-1981
1326.	Vojvodinha Novi Sad (Yug)	European Cup 1966-1967
1327.	Dinamo Kiev (Ukr)	European Cup 1967-1968
1328.	Red Star Belgrade (Yug)	European Cup 1968-1969
1329.	Ujpest Budapest (Yug)	European Cup 1971-1972
1330.	Kispest-Honved Budapest (Hun)	European Cup 1988-1989

EXPERT - THE "OLD FIRM"

1331.   Jimmy Quinn
1332.   The Drybrough Cup
1333.   George Livingstone
1334.   John Thomson
1335.   Celtic 7, Rangers 6 (also met in 1909 but, following riots, the SFA withdrew the trophy)
1336.   Billy McPhail
1337.   Willie Fernie (penalty), Neilly Mochan (2) & Sammy Wilson
1338.   1969 (Celtic won 4-0), 1971 (Celtic won 2-1 after a Replay) & 1973 (lost 3-2)
1339.   Harry Hood
1340.   Celtic 5 Rangers 2

EXPERT - SEASON 1999-2000

1341.   Aberdeen
1342.   Celtic 2 Aberdeen 0
1343.   3
1344.   58 (conceded 17)
1345.   8 (he broke his leg early in the season away to Lyon)
1346.   Tommy Johnson

1347.   9
1348.   32 (conceded 21)
1349.   St Johnstone
1350.   Hearts (conceded 40)

EXPERT - OPPOSITION

1351.   Wislaw Krakow (of Poland in the 1st Round)
1352.   Jeunesse d'Esch (1st Qualifying Round in 2000-2001)
1353.   Patrick Thistle (Celtic won 3-0 in 1957)
1354.   Politehnica Timisoara (1980-1981)
1355.   Sao Paulo FC
1356.   Bordeaux (2nd Round)
1357.   Leicester City
1358.   FC Barcelona (2nd Round)
1359.   FK Suduva, Blackburn Rovers, Celta Vigo, Stuttgart, Liverpool, Boavista & FC Porto
1360.   Xamax Neuchatel (2nd Round)

EXPERT - IF YOU KNOW YOUR HISTORY - PLAYERS

1361.   Reggie Blinker
1362.   Stephen Pearson
1363.   James McColl (34 goals)
1364.   Henrik Larsson (5), Brian McClair (2) & Charlie Nicholas (2)
1365.   Mathieson
1366.   Charlie Nicholas
1367.   David Hay
1368.   Paul Lambert (with Borussia Dortmund)
1369.   Joe McBride (No. 16) & Billy McNeill (No. 18)
1370.   Jimmy McGrory (49 goals & 50 goals respectively)

EXPERT - CHAMPIONS OF EUROPE

1371.   Jim Craig
1372.   West Germany (Kurt Techenscher)
1373.   Sandro Mazzola
1374.   Helenio Herrera
1375.   Bobby Murdoch
1376.   Zurich
1377.   Vojvodina Novi Sad (Yugoslavia)
1378.   Billy McNeill
1379.   Nantes
1380.   Celtic 6 Nantes 2

EXPERT - SEASON 2000-2001 - TREBLE WINNERS
1381. Hibernian
1382. Celtic 3 Hibernian 0
1383. 17
1384. 49 (conceded 11)
1385. 35
1386. Stilian Petrov
1387. 14
1388. 41 (conceded 18)
1389. Dundee
1390. Hibernian (conceded 35 - Rangers conceded 36)

EXPERT - SEASON 2004 - 2005
1391. Motherwell (Celtic won 2-0)
1392. Kilmarnock (4-2)
1393. Barcelona (in the UEFA Champions League on 14th September)
1394. Falkirk
1395. Aberdeen
1396. Shakhtar Donetsk
1397. Rangers 2 Celtic 1 (at Ibrox in the Scottish League Cup)i
1398. Hibernian (away on 19th September)
1399. 2-2
1400. Jackie McNamara (in the opening day 2-0 win over Motherwell)

EXPERT - CELTIC IN THE FAIRS/UEFA CUP
1401. 8 (1996-1997 to 2003-2004)
1402. Sporting Lisbon
1403. 4
1404. 1998-1999, 2001-2002, 2002-2003 & 2003-2004
1405. FC Barcelona & FC Villareal
1406. Valencia (1962-1963)
1407. Borussia Dortmund (1987-1988 & 1992-1993)
1408. 1.FC Cologne (1992-1993), SV Hamburg (1996-1997) & Stuttgart (2002-2003)
1409. Leixoes Matosinhos (1st Round in 1964-1965)
1410. Olympique Lyon (1999-2000) & Bordeaux (2000-2001)

EXPERT - PAST PLAYERS
1411. Pierre van Hooijdonk (Benfica, Celtic, Feyenoord & Nottingham Forest)
1412. Joe Kennoway (he also represented the Scottish League)
1413. John Divers (the Italian League won 4-3)

1414. Jim Welford (with Aston Villa in 1895 & with Celtic in 1899)
1415. John "Dixie" Deans (v. Hibernian in 1972 & 1975 respectively)
1416. Sandy McMahon (1899 v. Rangers & 1900 v. Queens' Park)
1417. John Madden (he also played for and managed Slavia Prague)
1418. Jimmy McGrory (1st with 410 goals) & Jimmy McColl (7th with 255 goals)
1419. Charlie Gallagher (against Turkey in 1967)
1420. Charlie Tully (his first goal was disallowed)

EXPERT - THE 1950s LEAGUE POSITIONS

1421. Season 1949-1950   5th
1422. Season 1950-1951   7th
1423. Season 1951-1952   9th
1424. Season 1952-1953   8th
1425. Season 1953-1954   1st
1426. Season 1954-1955   2nd
1427. Season 1955-1956   5th
1428. Season 1956-1957   5th
1429. Season 1957-1958   3rd
1430. Season 1958-1959   6th

EXPERT - IF YOU KNOW YOUR HISTORY - TRIVIA 3

1431. 2
1432. Southampton (On loan from Wolverhampton Wanderers)
1433. Kevin Keegan (he also replaced him as a player at Liverpool)
1434. 14 (Celtic 6 & Liverpool 7 & Blackburn Rovers 1)
1435. Rangers (beat Celtic 1-0 in the final)
1436. 230
1437. Stilian Petrov
1438. Charlie Nicholas
1439. 9 (1966-1967 to 1974-1975)
1440. 35

EXPERT - SEASON 2001-2002

1441. Rangers 3, Celtic 2
1442. 18 (drew 1)
1443. 94
1444. 29
1445. Shaun Maloney (5 league, 1 FA & 4 CIS)
1446. 4 (won 15, drew 3 & lost 1)
1447. 43 (conceded 9)
1448. Livingston

1449.   Aberdeen in 4th place (Hearts were 5th & Dundee United were 8th)
1450.   Valencia (3rd Round - lost 5-4 in a penalty shoot-out)

EXPERT - JOCK STEIN - THE LION KING
1451.   Albion Rovers (also played part-time for Blantyre Victoria Juniors)
1452.   1954
1453.   1960
1454.   The Scottish FA Cup (in 1961 with Dunfermline Athletic beating Celtic 2-0 in a Replay)
1455.   1964
1456.   6
1457.   1966 (plus 1967-1970 & 1975)
1458.   1975
1459.   Sean Fallon
1460.   The Glasgow Cup

EXPERT - JIMMY JOHNSTONE
1461.   Viewpark, Lanarkshire
1462.   Manchester United
1463.   Robert Duvall
1464.   Kilmarnock (27 March 1963)
1465.   308
1466.   4
1467.   5
1468.   No. 3
1469.   The Earth Team
1470.   16

EXPERT - SUPER KENNY
1471.   511
1472.   172
1473.   102
1474.   30
1475.   Denis Law
1476.   English First Division Championship (1985-1986)
1477.   1995
1478.   1977
1479.   4
1480.   1981, 1982, 1983 & 1984

EXPERT - SCOTTISH FA CUP FINAL VICTORIES - 2

1481.	Dunfermline 2004	3-1
1482.	Aidrieonians 1995	1-0
1483.	Rangers 1971 (Replay)	2-1
1484.	Hibernian 2001	3-0
1485.	Dundee United 1985	2-1
1486.	Dunfermline Athletic 1965	3-2
1487.	Rangers 1969	4-0
1488.	Motherwell 1931	4-2
1489.	Hibernian 1972	6-1
1490.	Rangers 1977	1-0

EXPERT - IF YOU KNOW YOUR HISTORY - TRIVIA - 4

1491. It was the last time Celtic started a league game with 11 Scottish-born players

1492. George Connelly (the Scottish League won 1-0)

1493. 12th

1494. Atletico de Madrid - European Cup Winners Cup tie on 2 October 1985 (an estimated 300 were in attendance as UEFA ordered Celtic to play the game behind closed doors following disturbances at the Rapid Vienna v. Celtic game the previous season)

1495. Celtic beat Raith Rovers 6-0 at home and Motherwell 3-1 away (15 April)

1496. Morton (at Celtic Park)

1497. 1968-1969

1498. The Drybrough Cup

1499. 1971 - Celtic beat Hearts 3-2

1500. Alex Boden (the Welsh League won 3-0)